CHRISTIANITY

A Journey from Facts to Fiction

Some Other Books by the Author

Absolute Justice, Kindness and Kinship

An Elementary Study of Islam

The Gulf Crisis and the New World Order

Homeopathy: Like Cures Like

Islam's Response to Contemporary Issues

Murder in the Name of Allah

Revelation, Rationality, Knowledge and Truth

CHRISTIANITY

A Journey from Facts to Fiction

MIRZA TAHIR AḤMAD
Khalifatul Masih IV
The Fourth Successor of the Promised Messiah

Christianity—A Journey from Facts to Fiction
  by Mirza Tahir Aḥmad

First published in U.K.   1994
Reprinted in UK in   1996, 1997, 2006, 2010
Present edition (UK)   2012

© Islam International Publications Ltd.
All Rights Reserved.

Published in the United Kingdom by:
Islam International Publications Ltd. Islamabad
Sheephatch Lane
Tilford, Surrey GUIO 2AQ

Printed and bound by CPI Group (UK) Ltd, Croydon, CR0 4YY

Cover design by Salman Sajid
Index prepared by Abdul Majid Shah

ISBN: 1 85372 883 7 (Hbk)

Ḥaḍrat Mirza Tahir Aḥmad   (1928–2003)
Khalifatul Masih IV
The Fourth Successor of the Promised Messiah

ABOUT THE AUTHOR

Ḥaḍrat Mirza Tahir Aḥmad[rh] (1928–2003), a man of God, Voice articulate of the age, a great orator, a deeply learned scholar of phenomenal intelligence, a prolific and versatile writer, a keen student of comparative religions was loved and devoutly followed by his more than 10 million Aḥmadi Muslim followers all over the world as their Imam, the spiritual head, being the fourth successor of Ḥaḍrat Mirza Ghulam Aḥmad (the Promised Messiah and Mahdi[as]), to which august office he was elected as Khalīfatul Masih in 1982.

After the promulgation of general Zia ul Ḥaq anti- Aḥmadiyya Ordinance of 26th April 1984 he had to leave his beloved country, Pakistan, and migrated to England from where he launched Muslim Television Aḥmadiyya International (MTA) which would (and still does) telecast its programmes 24 hours a day to the four corners of the world.

Besides being a religious leader, he was a homeopathic physician of world fame, a highly gifted poet and a sportsman.

He had his schooling in Qadian, India, and later joined the Govt. College, Lahore, Pakistan, and after graduating from Jami‘ah Aḥmadiyya, Rabwah, Pakistan with distinction, he obtained his honours degree in Arabic from the Punjab University, Lahore. From 1955 to 1957 he studied at the School of Oriental and African Studies, University of London.

He had a divinely inspired and very deep knowledge of the Holy Quran which he translated into Urdu. He also partially revised and added explanatory notes to the English translation of the Holy Quran by Hadrat Maulawi Sher 'Ali[ra]. 'Revelation, Rationality, Knowledge and Truth' is his magnum opus.

Though he had no formal education in philosophy and science, he had a philosophical bent of mind and tackled most difficult and abstruse theological-philosophical questions with great acumen and ease and his intellectual approach was always rational and scientific. For a layman he had an amazingly in-depth knowledge of science, especially life sciences which attracted him most He also had deep knowledge of human psychology. His was an analytical mind of high intelligence—an intellect scintillating with brilliance, capable of solving knottiest problems with ease, leaving his listeners and readers spellbound.

CONTENTS

FOREWORD
TO THE PRESENT EDITION

Christianity—A Journey from Facts to Fiction, by Ḥaḍrat Mirza Tahir Aḥmad, (1928–2003), Khalifatul Masih IV, was first published in U.K. in 1994 by Islam International Publication Ltd., and it is being reissued now.

The book is a critique of the fundamental tenets of Christianity, or to put it in modern philosophical terminology—used here loosely—it is a deconstruction of the myth of Christianity. The critique or the deconstruction is based on forceful, flawless and impeccable logical arguments to dismantle the myth so that its entire fabric is unravelled just in about two hundred pages. At the very outset the author, in his foreword, says: 'I have chosen to address the question solely from a logical point of view. I believe that this is the only platform, common to all, which can be used for a fruitful constructive dialogue. Otherwise any discussion on the basis of what the individual scriptures present, along with their various interpretations, would lead to a tangle of controversy from which it would be difficult to wriggle out.' When the author uses scriptural, scientific and historical evidence in the context of his discourse, he uses it only to develop his logical arguments which are his mainstay. Logic being his forte, no unprejudiced reader, Christian or non-Christian, would find himself able to defy his logic.

However, when the author explodes the myth of 'Christianity', he—God forbid—does not mean to be disrespectful to Jesus

Christ[as], or refute Christianity understood as the true teachings and examples of Jesus Christ[as]. He says: 'I must emphasize, however, that I do not mean to be disrespectful, in any way, to the Christians or to the person of Jesus Christ[as]. As a Muslim, it is a fundamental article of my faith to believe in the truth of Jesus Christ[as] and to accept him as a special and honoured Messenger[as] of God, holding a unique position among the Prophets of Israel.... My purpose is not to drive a wedge between Christians and Christ[as]. On the contrary, I wish to help Christians to come closer to the reality of Jesus Christ[as] and away from the myth created around him'

The Christian myth, according to the author, has led to the moral decadence of Christians and has helped promoting Western Imperialism. It has also been a hindrance in the progress of knowledge, especially scientific knowledge which was made possible only when the myth was renounced, with the unfortunate consequence of turning most Christian scholars, scientists and other intellectuals to atheism—in fact, it (the myth) turned Europe into a breeding ground of atheism.

Putting aside the myth and turning to facts, we find that Jesus Christ[as] was a man, and no more than a man, and a great Prophet of God. 'His real greatness lies in the fact that he transcended and conquered the forces of darkness that had conspired to vanquish him despite being a human being and no more than a human being. That victory of Jesus[as] is something to be shared with pride by the children of Adam[as]. He taught humanity by his example of perseverance in the face of extreme suffering and pain. Not to surrender but to remain steadfast in the teeth of extreme trial was the noblest achievement of Jesus[as]. It was his life of suffering and pain [not his fictional death on the cross to suffer for three days and nights in Hell] that redeemed humanity.' He did not voluntarily accept death: he conquered death.

I believe that this book needs to be read from cover to cover. The main theme of the book—the critique of Christian doctrines like the Godhead of Christ[as] his 'Resurrection' and 'Ascension' etc—is covered in the first six chapters. The seventh chapter traces the history of the evolution of Christianity. The last chapter— *Christianity Today*—is important in its own right and must not be skipped over. Its two main themes are: (1) the relationship of Christianity and the West and (2) prophecy about the second coming of Christ[as] which was fulfilled with the advent of the Promised Messiah, Ḥaḍrat Mirza Ghulam Aḥmad[as]. Analyzing the relationship of Christianity to the West, the author makes a very important observation and says: 'From the above it should be evident that the Christianity we are talking about is very distant from the Christianity of Jesus Christ[as]. To conceive of Western culture as Christianity is a manifest error. To attribute the current form of Christianity, in its various spheres, to Christ[as] is indeed an insult to him. There are exceptions of course to every rule... [Thus] there is a small number of individual islands of hope and life in the Christian world where Christian sincerity, love and sacrifice are genuinely practiced. There are the islands of hope around which rage oceans of immorality that are slowly and gradually corroding and finally claiming more edges of these islands. Had the Christian world not been bejewelled with such shining examples of Christianity practiced in the spirit of Jesus

Christ[as], however a few and far between, a total darkness would envelop the Western horizon. Without Christianity there is no light in Western civilization, but, alas, that light is also fast fading.

It is essential for the Christian world to return to the reality of Christ[as] and to cure themselves of their *split identity* and *inherent hypocricy*[*].'

Summing up the theme of the Coming of the first Messiah—Jesus Christ[as]—and his second Coming in the person of Ḥaḍrat Mirza Ghulam Aḥmad[as]. The author says: 'Here is the case of Messiah who was a fact of history and not the product of fiction, and here again is the case of Messiah whose re-advent was as realistic as was his first appearance as a commissioned Divine leader. It is entirely upto the people of this age to choose to live continuously in a world of legends and fancies… or to accept the hard realities of this life.'

As Muslims we believe in, deeply love and have the greatest regard for this Noble Prophet[as] of Allah Jesus Christ[as]. And as Aḥmadi Muslims we believe in his second coming which was fulfilled in the person of Ḥaḍrat Mirza Ghulam Aḥmad[as] the Promised Messiah and Mahdi. And we invite the whole world to Jesus Christ[as], the Prophet of Allah. We invite the entire world to the Holy Prophet Muhammad[sa], the last and the greatest Prophet[as] of Allah, about whose advent Jesus Christ[as], like other Prophets[as], prophesied. And we invite the whole world to Ḥaḍrat Mirza Ghulam Aḥmad[as], the Promised Messiah and Mahdi who was the

---

[*] Italics are mine.

true servant of the Holy Prophet Muhammad[sa], who was raised by Allah in the likeness of Jesus Christ[as] and who was sent by Allah to complete the mission of the Holy Prophet[sa]—the revival of Islam and its final victory over all other faiths and creeds.

May Allah guide and bless all.

Mirza Anas Aḥmad
M.A. M. Litt. (OXON)

Wakīlul Ishā'at,
Rabwah
Pakistan

PUBLISHER'S NOTE

We are pleased to publish the fourth edition of Christianity—a Journey from Facts to Fiction, by Ḥaḍrat Mirza Tahir Aḥmad[rh], which was first published in 1994.

Please note that all the Biblical references except one on page 125, are taken from the New Oxford Annotated Bible, with the Apocrypha, Revised Standard Versions, New York, Oxford University Press, 1973.

The name of Muhammad[sa], the Holy Prophet of Islam, has been followed by the symbol [sa], which is an abbreviation for the salutation (ﷺ) Ṣallallāhu 'Alaihi Wasallam (may peace and blessings of Allah be upon him). The names of other Prophets[as] and messengers are followed by the symbol [as], an abbreviation for (عليه السلام/عليهم السلام) 'Alaihissalām/'Alaihimussalām (on whom be peace). The actual salutations have not generally been set out in full, but they should nevertheless, be understood as being repeated in full in each case. The symbol [ra] is used with the name of the Companions of the Holy Prophet[sa] and those of the Promised Messiah[as]. It stands for (رضي الله عنه / رضي الله عنها / رضي الله عنهم) Raḍī Allāhu 'anhu/'anhā/'anhum (May Allah be pleased with him/with her/with them). [rh] stands for (رحمه الله) Rahimahullāhu Ta'ālā (may Allah's blessing be on him). [at] stands for (ايده الله) Ayyadahullāhu Ta'ālā (May Allah, the Almighty help him).

In transliterating Arabic words we have followed the following system adopted by the Royal Asiatic Society.

ا   at the beginning of a word, pronounced as *a, i, u* preceded by a very slight aspiration, like *h* in the English word 'honour'.

ث   *th*, pronounced like *th* in the English word 'thing'.

ح   *ḥ*, a guttural aspirate, stronger than *h*.

خ   *kh*, pronounced like the Scotch *ch* in 'loch'.

ذ   *dh*, pronounced like the English *th* in 'that'.

ص   *ṣ*, strongly articulated *s*.

ض   *ḍ*, similar to the English *th* in 'this'.

ط   *ṭ*, strongly articulated palatal *t*.

ظ   *ẓ*, strongly articulated *z*.

ع   ', a strong guttural, the pronunciation of which must be learnt by the ear.

غ   *gh*, a sound approached very nearly in the *r* '*grasseye*' in French, and in the German *r*. It requires the muscles of the throat to be in the 'gargling' position whilst pronouncing it.

ق   *q*, a deep guttural *k* sound.

ئ   ', a sort of catch in the voice.

Short vowels are represented by:

     a   for ——— (like *u* in 'bud');

     i   for ——— (like *i* in 'bid');

     u   for ——— (like *oo* in 'wood');

Long vowels by:

     a   for ——— or آ (like *a* in 'father');

     i   for ى ——— or ——— (like *ee* in 'deep');

     u   for و ——— (like *oo* in 'root');

Other:

ai   for ی ⸺⸺ (like *i* in 'site') ♦ ;

au   for و ⸺⸺ (resembling *ou* in 'sound').

Please note that in transliterated words the letter 'e' is to be pronounced as in 'prey' which rhymes with 'day'; however the pronunciation is flat without the element of English diphthong. If in Urdu and Persian words 'e' is lengthened a bit more it is transliterated as 'ei' to be pronounced as 'ei' in 'feign' without the element of diphthong thus 'کے' is transliterated as 'Kei'. For the nasal sound of 'n' we have used the symbol ' '. Thus Urdu word 'میں' is transliterated as 'mei'.*

The consonants not included in the above list have the same phonetic value as in the principal languages of Europe.

We have not transliterated Arabic words which have become part of English language, e.g., Islam, Mahdi, Quran**, Hijra, Ramadan, Hadith, ulama, umma, sunna, kafir, pukka etc.

Curved commas are used in the system of transliteration, ' for ع, ' for ء. Commas as punctuation marks are used according to the normal usage. Similarly for apostrophe normal usage is followed.

The Publishers

♦ In Arabic words like شیخ (Shaikh) there is an element of diphthong which is missing when the word is pronounced in Urdu.

* These transliterations are not included in the system of transliteration by Royal Asiatic Society. [Publisher]

** Concise Oxford Dictionary records Quran in three forms—Quran, Quran and Koran. [Publisher]

INTRODUCTION

The person of Christ[as] is vitally important to the contemporary world. His importance does not remain confined to the Christian world alone but also extends to other major religions such as Judaism and Islam in particular. If these powerful religions were to unite in one common understanding about the nature of the person of Christ[as], his first and also his promised second advent, then such an understanding would lead to the resolution of many problems confronting mankind today. Unfortunately, even the very basic facts about the life of Jesus[as], his purpose, ideology and person are completely misunderstood. In their perception of these aspects, these religions are so strongly at odds with each other that a bitter rivalry among them becomes inevitable.

When we look at the facts of Crucifixion and consider what happened and why it happened, as well as at Redemption and its related philosophy, we find conflicting answers from various early sources. I have chosen to address this question solely from a logical point of view. I believe that this is the only platform, common to all, which can be used for a fruitful constructive dialogue. Otherwise, any discussion on the basis of what the individual scriptures present, along with their various interpretations, would lead to a tangle of controversy from which it would be difficult to wriggle out.

Two thousand years have already come to pass, yet based on the scriptures alone, no solution which would be equally acceptable to all has so far been reached. The crux of the problem is that the very reliability of certain scriptural claims is further compounded by their various divergent explanations. Also, immense complications arise out of the gradual growth of conflicting understandings revolving around the historical person of Christ[as]. The vision of a historic perspective generally tends to be fogged and obscured. By any standards, the passage of two millennia is no ordinary obstacle in perceiving events as distant as that of the time of Jesus[as]. Human logic and reason, further aided by the dawn of scientific knowledge, have neither creed, nor colour nor religion. They are common to all peoples and religions alike. Logic and logic alone can provide us with a basis for consensus.

I will attempt to examine the problem from different vantage points. First, let me begin with Christianity and view it as the Christians see it and then critically analyse it under the magnifying glass of reason. I must emphasize, however, that I do not mean to be disrespectful, in any way, to the Christians or to the person of Jesus Christ[as]. As a Muslim, it is a fundamental article of my faith to believe in the truth of Jesus Christ[as], and to accept him as a special and honoured messenger of God, holding a unique position among the prophets of Israel. But where truth demands, in all fairness to logic, common sense and human understanding, one cannot abstain from revising one's views on Christianity. My purpose is not to drive a wedge between Christians and Christ[as]. On the contrary, I wish to help Christians come closer to the reality of Jesus Christ[as] and move away from the myth created around him.

Time can distort reality into myths and legends. The influence of such legends only serves to distance man from the realities of life. As a result, faith becomes imaginary and unreal. Whereas true faith has its roots in the verities and facts of history, it is very real and potent enough to bring about significant changes in human society.

In the endeavour to understand the true faith and teachings of Jesus[as], it is essential to sift out the fact from the fiction and truth from myth. The search for truth is the ultimate purpose of this exercise. I hope that you will bear with me and understand that I mean no offence to anyone's beliefs or sentiments.

A critical approach is essential to save the world of Christianity from unfortunate moral degradation—the course of which it is finding so hard to reverse. According to my analysis, contemporary youth is fast losing its faith in God. There was a time when scientists began moving away from God because they thought that the Judeo-Christian understanding of nature, as depicted in the Old and New Testaments, was not realistic. The understanding of the world and of the heavenly bodies and of what lies beyond, as construed from a study of the Bible, appears far removed from the realities of scientific discoveries brought to light at the beginning of the Renaissance. The parallax between them continued to grow as science progressed and the human understanding of nature underwent a revolutionary change. This, besides other factors, initiated among the knowledgeable factions of society, a fatal trend towards disbelief in God. Later, as education spread far and wide, great universities and seats of learning turned out to be the breeding grounds of Atheism. The dilemma of the Judeo-Christian understanding of the Universe was that there prevailed a contradiction between the word of God and the act of God. The argument against belief in God took the following course: If God is the Creator of the universe and all that belongs to it, and if He is the Designer and Maintainer of the laws of nature, as discovered by investigative human minds, then how could He Himself have been so utterly ignorant of those realities?

When one studies the Biblical account of how heaven and earth were created and how man was fashioned out of dust and how Eve was carved out of the rib of Adam etc. (two examples out of a host of puzzling discrepancies between the word and the act of God), one is astounded and amazed at the glaring contradictions between the origin of life on earth and the Biblical account given in Genesis.

Such inconsistencies made the Church take an oppressive stance in those times when it held an unchallenged political authority. One famous example is that of the tussle between the Church and Galileo. When Galileo (1564–1642) published his findings about the solar system, it infuriated the Church because his findings were against the perception which the Church had of the solar system. Under extreme duress he was forced to publicly renounce his scientific discoveries. Alternatively he would have suffered death by torture. Nevertheless, he was kept under house arrest for the rest of his days. It was only in 1992 that the Church decided to reverse the judgement passed against Galileo, after prolonged deliberations that lasted twelve years by a committee set up by the Pope, John Paul II.

To begin with, the impact of these contradictions did not penetrate or infiltrate the common levels of society and for some time it remained confined to a close circle of intellectuals. But with the spread of the light of secular knowledge, the so-called 'light of religious beliefs' gradually diminished into comparative darkness. In the early period of the Renaissance (15th Century), the activities of scientists generally remained confined within their own enlightened circles. A broad contact between them and the general public, as witnessed today, had not been established. Thus, their atheism did not much influence the society as a whole. However, when universal education was made available to the youth of advanced nations, things began to swiftly change in the wrong direction for religion. There followed an age of philosophy and rationality. Along with the sciences, new social and psychological philosophies began to proliferate rapidly, particularly in the nineteenth and the twentieth centuries.

As the new materialistic philosophies mingled with secular development and thought, they played havoc with the very foundation of religion, i.e. the belief in God. Morality is always governed and safeguarded by his belief in God. If this belief is weak and deficient or there is something amiss in it, then morality is influenced to the same degree. If for instance, the belief in God clashes with the secular understanding of nature and the dictates of common sense, then slowly and progressively the quality of people's faith in God erodes with a correspondingly negative effect on their morals. For all practical purposes a society is then transformed into an atheistic one, however much individuals may remain believers in God. It is not difficult to determine this issue and to ascertain the quality of a society's belief in God. The weaker the belief or the more deficient it is, the feebler its hold becomes on the moral conduct of a people. Whenever the two interests clash, the belief in God will give way to immoral urges.

By applying this criterion to any religious society anywhere in the world, we can always draw correct and reliable conclusions. Putting a so-called believing Christian society to the test, one can simply ask whether Christian values prevail in that society or not. Do they, for instance, behave towards their neighbours as the Ten Commandments would require of them? Do they, at the time of national crisis in situations of war etc., apply Christian principles towards their adversaries? Do the innocent victims of aggression and assault offer the other cheek when smitten on one? The question is how far does one's conduct in life portray the picture of one's belief? If it does not, this is exactly what we mean by suggesting that the belief in God clashes with human urges and requirements. If the belief in God stands supreme and it is the human urges and desires that are sacrificed on the altar of that belief, then one can truly say that whatever the nature of the belief, at least it is genuine, sincere and strong.

Observing the world of Christianity as it is today, and applying this test to judge the quality of belief in God becomes a very depressing and disillusioning experience. What is generally seen is an open rebellion against the belief in God, and sometimes a passive revolt which is not translated into open negation. It is the contradiction between the belief in God and the practices of individuals, which gives one the illusion of there being a religious society of believers, while the truth is very different. The same applies, to a large degree, to all other religious societies. But in every case it is not always the same cause which produces a similar effect. The case of each society has to be dealt with on the merits of that case. That is why a genuine, detached, cool and analytical examination of the nature of the contradictions between the beliefs of people and their practices acquires such importance.

It is important to note that sometimes belief in itself is crooked and unnatural. For example, some parts of the Talmudic teachings concerning the Gentiles and the Hindu teachings of *Manu Samarti*[*] regarding the Untouchables are such that it becomes a boon for those societies not to practice them. Sometimes a belief in itself is good and would be beneficial if practised, but the people become corrupt and the belief is abandoned as too difficult and demanding to be taken seriously.

Returning to the question of Christianity, we propose that the Christian beliefs in their fundamentals clash with the realities of nature and do not comply with human expectations based on rationality and common sense. With this perspective, it was only natural for Christians to gradually move away from taking their beliefs seriously and from permitting those beliefs to shape their lives.

---

[*] A book by Manu, a Hindu saint. [Publishers]

CHAPTER ONE

THE SONSHIP OF JESUS CHRIST

THE 'FATHER-SON' RELATIONSHIP BETWEEN GOD and Jesus Christ[as] is central to Christianity. Let us first try to understand the meaning of being a literal son. When we concentrate on the meaning of being a literal son to a literal father, things begin to appear which force us to revise our opinion of 'sonship' of Jesus[as]. What is a son? During the period when science had not yet developed and discovered how a child is born, this question could only be vaguely answered. Ancient people thought it quite possible for God to have a son through human birth. This was a belief prevalent in almost all pagan societies in different parts of the world. Greek mythology abounds with such tales and Hindu mythology does not lag far behind either. For the so-called gods to have sons and daughters, as many as they pleased, was in fact never seriously challenged by human reason. But now science has developed to a stage where the process of human birth has been described in greater detail than ever before. This issue has become very complicated and those who still believe that literal sons and daughters can be born to God have very serious problems to resolve and some very difficult questions to answer.

The Scientific Basis of Parenthood

First of all, let me remind you that the mother and father participate equally in producing a child. The cells of human beings contain 46 chromosomes, which carry the genes or character-bearing threads of life. The ovum of a human mother possesses only 23 chromosomes. This is half the total number of chromosomes found in each man and woman. When the mother's ovum is ready and available for insemination, the other half of the chromosomes which it lacks is provided by the male sperm, which then enters and fertilizes it. This is the design of God; otherwise, the number of chromosomes would begin to double with every generation. As a result of this doubling the second generation would have 92 chromosomes; humans would soon be transformed into giants and the entire process of growth would run amok. God has so beautifully planned and designed the phenomenon of the survival of species that at productive levels of regenerative cells, chromosomes are halved in number. The mother's ovum contains 23 chromosomes and so does the father's sperm. As such, one can reasonably expect half the character-bearing genes of the child to be provided by the female and half by the male partner. This is the meaning of literal son. There is no other definition of a literal son, which can be ascribed to any human birth. There are variations in the methodology of course, but there are no exceptions to the rules and principles just explained.

Focusing our attention on the birth of Jesus[as], let us build a scenario about what might have happened in his case. The first possibility which can be scientifically considered is that Mary's[as] unfertilized ovum provided the 23 chromosomes as the mother's share in the forming of the embryo. That being so, the question would arise as to how the ovum was fertilized and where the remaining 23 essential chromosomes came from? It is impossible to suggest that Jesus'[as] cells had only 23 chromosomes. No normal human child can be born alive with even 45 chromosomes. Even if a human being was deprived of a single chromosome out of the 46 necessary for the making of normal human being, the result would be something chaotic, if anything at all. Scientifically, Mary[as] could not provide the 46 chromosomes alone; 23 had to come from somewhere else.

If God is the father then that presents several options. One, God also has the same chromosomes that humans have, in which case these must have been transferred somehow to the uterus of Mary[as]. That is unbelievable and unacceptable; if God has the chromosomes of human beings He no longer remains God. So as a consequence of belief in Jesus[as] as the literal 'Son' of God, even the divinity of the Father is jeopardised.

The second possibility is that God created the extra chromosomes as a supernatural phenomenon of creation. In other words, they did not actually belong to the person of God, but were created miraculously. This would automatically lead us to reject Jesus'[as] relationship to God as one of child to father, and would result in the all-embracing relationship of the Universe to God, that is, the relationship of every created being to its Creator.

Is a Literal Son of God Possible?

Evidently, therefore, literal sonship of God is impossible because a literal son must have half the chromosomes of his father and half the chromosomes of his mother. So another problem surfaces, the son would be half man and half god. But those who believe in literal sonship, claim and emphasise that Christ[as] was a perfect man and a perfect god.

If the chromosomes were half the required number then we are not left with any problem, since no child would be born anyway. suppose it did happen, that child would only be half a man. Not to mention the missing twenty three full chromosomes, even a single defective gene within one chromosome can play havoc with a child born with such a congenital defect. He could be blind, limbless, deaf and dumb. The dangers attendant to such a mishap are unlimited. One should be realistic; it is impossible to conceive of God as possessing any chromosomes, human or otherwise.

Therefore, with the personal physical contribution of God having been ruled out, if a son were born to Mary[as] with only the human character-bearing genes possessed by her ovum, whatever the outcome, he would certainly not be the 'Son' of God. At best you could describe that freak of nature as half a man and no more. If the reproductive organs of Mary[as] were like those of any other female and still the ovum were to fertilize somehow by itself, the maximum one can expect is the creation of something with only half the human characteristics. It would be abominable to call that something the 'Son' of God.

So how was Christ[as] born? We understand that research on the subject of single mother birth without the participation of a male is being carried out in many advanced countries of the world. But so far human knowledge is only at a stage where scientific research has not yet advanced to such a level where positive irrefutable evidence of virgin births in human beings can be produced. However, all sorts of possibilities remain open.

At lower orders of life two phenomena are scientifically well established: Hermaphroditism and Parthenogenesis. As such, the miraculous birth of Jesus[as] to Mary[as] can be understood to belong to some similar natural but very rare phenomenon, the peripheries of which are not yet fully fathomed by man.

Here follow brief descriptions of the phenomena of Hermaphroditism and Parthenogenesis. Readers interested in a more scientific treatment of the subject matter, based upon current understanding, may refer to Appendix II.

Hermaphroditism

Hermaphroditism exists when organs of both sexes are present within a single female and the chromosomes show both male and female characters aligned side by side. Laboratory tests have revealed cases such as that of a hermaphrodite rabbit which, at one stage, served several females and sired more than 250 young of both sexes, while at another stage, it became pregnant in isolation and gave birth to seven healthy young of both sexes. When autopsied, it, while in a pregnant condition, showed two functional ovaries and two infertile testes. Recent studies suggest that such a phenomenon is possible, rarely, among humans also.

Parthenogenesis

Parthenogenesis is the asexual development of a female ovum into an individual, without the aid of a male agent. It is observed among many lower forms of life such as aphids and also fish. There is also evidence that parthenogenesis can be a successful strategy among lizards living under low and unpredictable rainfall conditions. In laboratory conditions, mice and rabbit embryos have been developed parthenogenetically to a stage equivalent to halfway through pregnancy, but have then been aborted. In a recent study, scientists found that human embryos could be occasionally activated by parthenogenesis using calcium ionophore as a catalyst. Such research raises the prospect that some early human pregnancy losses may have involved the parthenogenetic activation of the embryo.

According to the latest experimental research, however, the possibility of virgin birth has been shown to be scientifically feasible. A report in the *Nature Genetics* of Oct. 1995 discusses the remarkable case of a three year old boy whose body is derived in part from an unfertilised egg. The researchers examined DNA sequences all along the X chromosomes in the boy's skin and blood and discovered that the X chromosomes in all his cells were identical to each other and derived entirely from his mother. Similarly, both members of each of the 22 other chromosome pairs in his blood were identical and derived entirely from his mother.

What are Miracles?

With the possibility of virgin birth being wide open, it does not remain to be all that impossible and unnatural. Where is the need to search for a supernatural explanation of Jesus'[as] birth, or to even go beyond that to the farthest extreme of believing in the birth of a literal 'Son' of God through human birth? When various phenomena, as described above, are observed as a fact of nature, why is it hard to believe that the birth of Jesus Christ[as] was a hidden natural phenomenon, brought about by a special design of God? Something happened in Mary[as] which gave that child a miraculous birth, without a man having touched her. It is the Aḥmadiyya Muslim belief that this is exactly what happened. Our case is unshakeable because no scientist can dismiss it as nonsensical or opposed to the known laws of nature.

Miracles are not seen in Islam as unnatural occurrences, but as natural phenomena that are concealed from human knowledge at a certain period of time. Otherwise, there would be many questions raised against the wisdom of God. If God created the laws of nature Himself, He should have made some provisions whereby without breaking them, He could bring about desired solutions to a problem.

Not all laws are known to man. There are categories of laws working as if in different tiers and on separate planes. Sometimes they are known to man only on one plane and man's sight is not able to penetrate beyond. As time goes on, man's knowledge increases and so does the penetration of man's sight and his capacity to observe such laws as had hitherto remained unperceived. As science progresses, new discoveries throw more light on such laws which seem to work in groups. So, their function and interaction with other laws is better understood.

Those things that appeared to be miracles in the early ages are no longer considered so. Miracles are so, only in relation to man's knowledge in a specific period of time. When a special exercise of God's power is displayed, apparently a law is broken. But it is not so; actually a hidden law was already there and only came into operation through God's command. The people of that time could not have understood that law, nor had they any control over it. For example, the force of magnetism was not known to man a few thousand years ago. If somebody had accidentally discovered it and had contrived a device by which he could levitate things without any apparent cause discernible to the naked eye then, to the wonderment of everyone, he could exclaim, 'Lo! A miracle has happened.' Today, such tricks are considered commonplace and trivial. The knowledge of man is limited whereas that of God is unlimited. If a law comes into operation that is beyond the scope of man's knowledge, it looks like a miracle. But looking retrospectively at such instances with the hindsight of knowledge gained since then, we can dismiss all such so-called breaches of the laws of nature as merely natural phenomena which were not fully comprehended by the man of that age. This is why I said that there had to be a natural phenomenon responsible for the single parent birth of Jesus Christ[as] which was unknown to man of that period; it is not fully known to man even today. But science is advancing in that direction and more is being understood. A time may therefore come, when no one will be able to claim that the birth of Jesus[as] was unnatural. They would have to agree that it was a natural but rare occurrence, so rare that it seldom occurs in human experience.

Jesus, the Son of God?

There are many other problems with the Christian understanding of Jesus[as], his nature and his relationship with God. From further critical and analytical study of Christian doctrine what emerges is that there is a 'Son of God' who possesses the characteristics of a perfect man and also those of a perfect God. However, remember that even according to Christian doctrine the Father is not exactly like the 'Son'. The Father God is a perfect God and not a perfect man, while the 'Son' is both a perfect man and a perfect god. In that case these are two separate personalities with different characteristics.

It should be realised that these characteristics are not transferable. There are characters in certain substances which are transferable. For instance, water can become snow and also vapour, without causing a change in the substance or composition of water. But the differences in the characteristics of God and Christ[as], where certain characteristics are added to one of them, are irreconcilable. It is not possible for one of them to go through this transformation and still remain indistinguishable from the other. It, again, is a problem, and a serious one for that matter, whether Jesus Christ[as] was a perfect god as well as a perfect man.

If he possessed both characteristics simultaneously, then he was surely different from the Father who was neither a perfect man nor even an imperfect one. What type of relationship was this? Was the 'Son' greater than the 'Father'? If this additional character did not make the 'Son' greater, then it must have been a defect. In that case a defective 'Son God' is not only against the claims of Christianity, but is also against the universal understanding of God. How, therefore, could anyone comprehend the paradoxical tenet of Christianity which would have us believe that 'One in Three' and 'Three in One' are the same thing, with no difference whatsoever? This can only happen when the very foundation of a belief is raised, not on a factual basis, but merely on myth.

Yet another problem to be resolved is this: if Jesus[as] became the 'Son of God' as a consequence of his birth from Mary's[as] womb, then what was his position before that? If he was eternally the 'Son', without having been born of Mary[as], why was it necessary to give birth to him in a human form? If it was necessary, then the quality of Son was not eternal; it only became an added character-istic after he was given birth to, and, it disappeared when he rejected the body and returned to heaven. So there are many complexities rising out of a belief which common sense rejects. I invite you again to accept a far more respectable and realistic scenario: that of believing the birth of Jesus Christ[as] to be a special creation brought about by God, who activated some hidden laws of nature. Jesus[as] was the metaphorical son of God, loved by Him in a special way, but a human being all the same. His 'Son' status was attached to his character some three hundred years later, to allow his legend to live on—this will be discussed later. The nature of the nuptial relationship between God the Father and Mary[as] is an issue which one loathes to discuss barefaced. Yet in an attempt to understand the intermediary role of Mary[as] between the 'Father' and the 'Son' this is an unavoidable evil. Perhaps it is the same question which bothered Nietzsche so much that he gave vent to his pent up dissatisfaction, at last, in the following words:

Not long after Zarathustra had freed himself from the sorcerer,
however, he again saw someone sitting beside the path he was going:
a tall, dark man with a pale, haggard face; this man greatly vexed
him. 'Alas,' he said to his heart, 'there sits disguised affliction, he
seems to be of the priestly sort: what do they want in my
kingdom?'... 'Whoever you may be, traveller', he said, 'help one
who has gone astray, an old man who may come to harm here!'

The world here is strange and remote to me, and I hear the howling
of wild animals; and he who could have afforded me protection is
himself no more.

I was seeking the last pious man, a saint and hermit who, alone in
the forest, had as yet heard nothing of what all the world knows
today.

'What does all the world know today?' asked Zarathustra. 'This
perhaps, that the old God in whom all the world once believed no
longer lives?'

'That is so', answered the old man sadly. 'And I served that old God until his last hour. Now, however, I am retired from service, without master, and yet I am not free, neither am I merry even for an hour, except in memories.'

'That is why I climbed into these mountains, that I might at last celebrate a festival once more, as becomes an old pope and church-father: for know, I am the last pope!—a festival of pious memories and divine services.'

'But now he himself is dead, the most pious of men, that saint in the forest who used continually to praise his God with singing and muttering.'

'When I found his hut I no longer found him himself, but I did find two wolves in it, howling over his death—for all animals loved him. Then I hurried away. Had I come into these forests and mountains in vain? Then my heart decided to seek another, the most pious of all those who do not believe in God—to seek Zarathustra!'

Thus spoke the old man and gazed with penetrating eyes at him who stood before him; Zarathustra, however, took the old pope's hand and for a long time regarded it admiringly.

*'Behold, venerable man', he said then, 'What a long and beautiful hand! It is the hand of one who has always distributed blessings. But now it holds fast him you seek, me, Zarathustra, It is **I,** the godless Zarathustra, the same who says: Who is more godless than **I,** that I may rejoice in his teaching?'*

Thus spoke Zarathustra and pierced with his glance the thoughts and reservations of the old pope. At last the latter began: 'He who loved and possessed him most, he has now lost him the most also, behold, am I myself not the more Godless of us too now? But who could rejoice in that! You served him to the last', asked Zarathustra thoughtfully, after a profound silence, 'do you know how he died? Is it true what they say that pity choked him, that he saw how man hung on the Cross and could not endure it, that love for man became his Hell and at last his death?' The old pope, however, did not answer, but looked away shyly and with a pained and gloomy expression.

'Let me go', said Zarathustra after prolonged reflection, during which he continued to gaze straight in the old man's eye. 'Let him go, he is finished. And although it honours you that you speak only good of this dead god, yet you know as well as I who he was; and that he followed strange paths.' 'Between ourselves', said the old pope, becoming cheerful, 'or, as I may say, spoken beneath the eyes' (for he was blind in one eye) 'in divine matters I am more enlightened than Zarathustra himself—and may well be so.'

'My love served him long years, my will obeyed all his will. A good servant, however, knows everything, and many things, too, that his master hides from himself.'

'He was hidden god, full of secrecy. Truly, he even came by a son through no other than secret and indirect means. At the door of faith in him stands adultery. Whoever honours him as the god of love

does not think highly enough of love itself. Did this God not also want to be judged? But the lover loves beyond reward and punishment. When he was young, this god from the orient, he was hard and revengeful and built himself a Hell for the delight of his favourites. But at length he grew old and soft and mellow and compassionate more like a grandfather than a father, most like a tottery old grandmother. Then he sat, shrivelled, in his chimney comer, fretting over his weak legs, world-weary, weary willing, and one day suffocated through his excessive pity.'

---

* Thus Spake Zarathustra, by Friedrich Nietzsche, p: 271–273 Translation published by Penguin Books 1969

CHAPTER TWO

SIN AND ATONEMENT

Now we turn to the second very important article of Christian faith. I must clarify, however, that all Christians do not believe exactly in what follows. Even some Church leaders have deviated from the stiff dogmatic attitude of the Church. Even so, the philosophy of 'Sin and Atonement' is a fundamental principle of orthodox Christian faith.

The first component of the Christian understanding of Sin and Atonement is that God is just, and exercises natural justice. He does not forgive sins without exacting retribution; as it would be against the dictates of absolute justice. It is this particular attribute of God that makes necessary the Christian version of atonement.

The second component is that man is sinful because Adam and Eve sinned. As a result their progeny began to inherit sin, as if it was infused into their genes and, ever since, all children of Adam are born congenital sinners.

The third component of this dogma is that a sinful person cannot atone for another person's sins: only a sinless person can do so. Based on this, it becomes evident that why according to Christian understanding, no Prophet[as] of God, however good or near perfection he may have been, could have cleansed mankind of sin or was able to rid them of it and its consequences. Being a son of Adam, he could not have escaped the element of congenital sin with which he was born.

This is a simple outline of the entire doctrine. Here is the solution advanced by Christian theologists.

The Atonement of Mankind

To solve this apparently insoluble problem, God conceived an ingenious plan. It is not clear as to whether He consulted His 'Son': did they both conceive the plan, or was it entirely the idea of the 'Son', which was later accepted by God the Father? The features of this plan unfolded at the time of Christ[as] are as follows: two thousand years ago the 'Son of God', who literally shared eternity with Him, was born to a human mother. As the 'Son of God', he combined within him the perfect traits of a human being as well as those of God the Father. Next we are told that a pious and chaste lady, by the name of Mary[as], was chosen to be the mother of the 'Son of God'. She conceived Jesus[as] in partnership with God. In that respect, being a literal 'Son of God', Jesus[as] was born without sin, yet somehow he retained his human character and entity. Thus he volunteered himself to take the burden of the entire sin of those of mankind who would believe in him and accept him as their saviour. By this clever device, it is claimed, God avoided compromising His eternal attribute of absolute justice.

Remember that according to this modus operandi man would not go unpunished, however sinful he might be. God would still be able to exact retribution from the sinful without compromising

His sense of justice. The only difference between this and the previous position, which was responsible for this dramatic change, is the fact that it would be Jesus[as] who would be punished and not the sinful sons and daughters of Adam. It would be the sacrifice of Jesus[as] which would ultimately be instrumental in atoning for the sins of the children of Adam. However strange and bizarre this logic may seem to be, this is exactly what is professed to have happened. Jesus[as] volunteered himself and was consequently punished for sins he had never committed.

The Sin of Adam and Eve

Let us re-examine the story of Adam from the beginning. Not a single step in the above doctrine can be accepted by human conscience and logic.

Firstly, we have the idea that because Adam and Eve sinned, their progeny became genetically and eternally polluted with sin. In contrast to this, the science of genetics reveals that human thoughts and actions, be they good or bad, even if persistently adhered to during the entire lifetime of a person, cannot be transferred to and encoded into the genetic system of human reproduction. A lifespan is too short a period to play any role in bringing about such profound changes. Even the vices of a people, generation after generation, or their good deeds for that matter, cannot be transferred to the progeny as genetic characters. Perhaps millions of years are required for etching human genes with new characteristics.

Even if by a most absurd and unacceptable extension of one's imagination one could conceive of such a bizarre happening, the contrary would also have to be accepted by the same logic. This would mean that if a sinful person repented and came out clean at the end of the day, then that act should also be recorded in the genetic system, effectively cancelling out the effect of the previous sin. Scientifically this may not happen, but certainly there is far more logic in this balanced picture than imagining that it is only the propensity to sin which can be genetically encoded and not the disposition to do good.

Secondly, by attempting to resolve the problem of Adam by proposing that sin is genetically transferred to the future generations of Adam, all that has been achieved is the total demolition of the very foundation on which the Christian doctrine of 'Sin and Atonement' is based. If God is absolutely Just, then where is the sense of justice in eternally condemning the entire progeny of Adam and Eve for the transient sin they committed and repented? This was, after all, a sin for which they themselves were heavily punished and driven out of heaven in such disgrace. What manner of justice would it be for God, Who, after more than punishing Adam and Eve for their personal sins, still did not have His passion of revenge abated and condemned the entire human race to a helpless degradation of being born congenital sinners? What chance did the children of Adam have to escape sin? If parents make a mistake why should their innocent children suffer for that mistake eternally?

That being so, what distorted sense of justice does God claim to possess and to enjoy, if He punishes a people who are designed to act sinfully, however much they abhor sin? Sin is made a part and parcel of their mechanism. There is no chance any more for a child of Adam to remain innocent. If sin were a crime, then logic demands that it should be a crime of the Creator and not that of the creation. In that case, what justice could require the punishment of the innocent for the crimes of the perpetrator?

How different from the Christian understanding of sin and its consequences is the proclamation of the Holy Quran, which says:

$$\ldots\ldots وَلَا تَزِرُ وَازِرَةٌ وِّزْرَ اُخْرٰى$$

No one can bear the burden of another... (The Holy Quran 35:19)

$$\ldots\ldots لَا يُكَلِّفُ اللّٰهُ نَفْسًا اِلَّا وُسْعَهَا$$

God requires not of anyone that which is beyond his capacity... (The Holy Quran 2:287)

Compared to the Christian concept of Sin and Atonement these declarations of the Holy Quran are pure music to the soul.

Let us now turn to the Biblical account of what actually happened at the time of the sin of Adam and Eve and the consequences that ensued upon their punishment. According to Genesis, God accepted their apology only partially and an eternal punishment was meted out to them, prescribed as follows:

To the woman he said, "I will greatly multiply your pain in childbearing; in pain you shall bring forth children, yet your desire shall be for your husband, and he shall rule over you."

And to Adam he said, "Because you have listened to the voice of
your wife, and have eaten of the tree of which I commanded you,
'You shall not eat of it,' cursed is the ground because of you; in toil
you shall eat of it all the days of your life; thorns and thistles it shall
bring forth to you; and you shall eat the plants of the field. In the
sweat of your face you shall eat bread till you return to the ground,
for out of it you were taken; you are dust, and to dust you shall
return." (Genesis 3:16–19)

Mankind existed long before Adam and Eve came to be born.
Western scientists themselves discovered the remains of many a
prehistoric man and labelled them under different distinctive titles.
Neanderthal man is perhaps the most widely known of them.
Neanderthals lived between 100,000 to 40,000 years ago, mostly
in the regions of Europe, Near East and Central Asia. A carcass of
a fully developed human being has been discovered, who happened to roam the earth about 29,000 years before Adam and Eve
are known to have begun their short lived sojourn in paradise. At
that time, human beings were physically just like us and lived in
Europe, Africa and Asia, and later during the Ice Age they spread
to the Americas as well. Again in Australia, the authentic cultural
history of Aborigines is traceable up to 40,000 years ago.

Compared to these relatively recent times, a skeleton of a female from Hedar in Western Ethiopia has been discovered which
is 2.9 million years old. Now according to the Biblical chronol-
ogy, Adam and Eve lived around six thousand years ago. One
may look back in wonderment at the reported history of human
beings, or Homo Sapiens as they are titled in scientific jargon.

Human Suffering Continues

Having read the Biblical account of how Adam and Eve were punished, one cannot help wondering if the pains and throes of labour were unknown to women until the beginning of the era of Adam and Eve. A scientist will be hard to come by who believes in such fantasies. Again, we have plenty of irrefutable evidence that long before Adam and Eve man had occupied all the continents of the world, even remote Pacific Islands, and had always laboured hard to survive. Therefore, to say that Adam and Eve were the first to commit a sin and because of that, painful childbirth was ordained as punishment is totally proven wrong by the study of life. Even animals, who are much lower in the order of life, give birth in pain. If one watches a cow giving birth to a calf, her suffering seems similar to the pain of a human female. Many such animals, we know, inhabited the earth millions and millions of years before Adam and Eve.

To earn one's livelihood with labour is common to man, but not distinctive at all. Women also labour for their earnings and livelihood. Before that, every species of life earns its livelihood through labour. This fact is the key motivator in the evolution of life. The struggle for existence is perhaps the very first distinctive mark of life which separates it from the world of the inanimate. It is a natural phenomenon, with nothing whatsoever to do with sin.

Again, if this be the punishment prescribed as a consequence of Adam and Eve's sin, then one wonders what would happen after Atonement. If Jesus Christ[as] had atoned for the sins of sinful human beings, was the punishment prescribed for the Sin of

Adam and Eve abolished after the Crucifixion? Did those who believed in Jesus Christ[as] as the 'Son of God,' if they were women, cease to have painful childbirth? Did the believing men start earning their livelihood without exerting themselves to manual labour? Did the propensity to sin cease to pass on to the future generations and innocent children started being given birth to? If the answer to all of these questions were to be 'yes', then of course there would be some justification in seriously contemplating the Christian philosophy of Sin and Atonement. But alas, the answer to all these questions is no, no and no. If nothing seems to have changed since the Crucifixion, both in the Christian and non-Christian worlds, then what are the meanings of Atonement?

Even after Jesus Christ[as] the sense of common justice continues to dictate to human beings all over the world that if any person commits a sin, punishment of that sin has to be given to that person alone and to none else. All men and women must suffer the consequences of their sins by themselves. Children are always born innocent. If this is not the truth then God's attribute of Justice is thrown overboard.

We as Muslims believe that all Divine books are based on eternal truth and none can make any claims contrary to that. When we come across inconsistencies and contradictions in any so-called Divinely revealed book, our attitude is not that of total denial and rejection but that of cautious and sympathetic examination. Most of the statements of the Old Testament and the New Testament, which we find at variance with the truth of nature, we either try to reconcile by reading some underlying cryptic or metaphoric message, or reject part of the text as the work of human hands rather than that of God. While Christianity itself was true, it could not have contained any distortions, unacceptable facts or beliefs giving a lie to nature. That is why we started not with textual examination but with the fundamentals themselves, which through centuries of consensus have become indisputable components of Christian philosophy. Rudimentary among them is the Christian understanding of Sin and Atonement. I would much rather believe that someone, somewhere during the history of Christianity, misunderstood things and tried to interpret them in the light of his knowledge and misled the following generations because of that.

Inherited Sin

Let us suppose for the sake of argument that Adam and Eve sinned literally as described in the Old Testament, and were duly punished. As the story goes, the punishment was handed out not only to them but to their entire progeny. Once that punishment was prescribed and delivered, why was there the need for any other punishment at all? Once a sin has been punished, it is done with. Once a judgement has been passed, no one has the right to continuously add more and more punishments. In the case of Adam and Eve it is not only that they were severely reprimanded, and if anything more than punished for the sin they had committed, but also the nature of the punishment which was extended to their progeny is in itself highly questionable. Of that we have said enough. What we are attempting to point to is a far more heinous violation of absolute justice. To be punished continuously for the sins of our forefathers is one thing but to be compelled to continue to sin as a consequence of one's forefather's error is simply abominable.

Let us get down to the hard realities of human experience and try to understand the Christian philosophy of crime and punishment in relation to our everyday experience. Let us suppose a judgement is passed against a criminal, which is far too severe and harsh in proportion to the crime committed. That could, of course, lead to loud and severe condemnation of such a gross disproportionate penalty by every sensible man. In view of this, we find it very difficult to believe that the penalty imposed on Adam for his sin came from a Just God. It is not just a case of an out of proportion penalty. It is a penalty that, according to the Christian understanding of God's conduct, outlived the lifespan of Adam and Eve and was extended generation after generation to their progeny. For the progeny to suffer for the punishment of their parents is actually an extension of the violation of justice beyond its ultimate limits. But we are not talking of that either. If we had the misfortune to observe a judgement passed by any contemporary judge making it compulsory for the children, grandchildren and great-grandchildren, etc. of a criminal to be coerced by law to continue to sin and commit crimes and be punished accordingly till eternity then what would be the reaction of contemporary society, which has acquired a universal sense of justice through civilisation?

The reader must be reminded here that this concept of inherited sin is only a Pauline misinterpretation. It cannot be rightfully attributed to the teachings of the Old Testament. There is overwhelming evidence to the contrary in many books of the Old Testament.

In the fifth century, Augustine, the Bishop of Hippo, was involved in a confrontation with the Pelagian[2] movement, concerning the controversy of the nature of the fall of Adam and Eve. He proclaimed the Pelagian movement as being heretical because it taught that Adam's sin affected only him and not the human race as a whole, that every individual is born free of sin and is capable in his own power of living a sinless life, and that there had even been persons who had succeeded in doing so.

Those in the right were labelled as heretics. Day was denounced as night, and night as day. Heresy is truth, and truth heresy.

The Transfer of Sin

Let us now re-examine the theme that God does not forgive the sinful without punishing them because it is against His sense of justice. One is horrified to realise that for century after century Christians have believed in something which is most certainly beyond the grasp of the human intellect and contrary to human conscience. How on earth, could God forgive a sinful person

---

[2] The movement of Pelagians, 360-420 CE. The British theologian. He taught that each person possesses free will (and hence the possibility of salvation), denying Augustines' doctrines of predestination and original sin. Cleared of heresy by a synod in Jerusalem 415, he was later condemned by the Pope and the emperor. [Publishers]

merely because an innocent person has volunteered himself to take the punishment instead? The moment God does so, He violates the very fundamental principles of justice. A sinful person must suffer for his sins. In short, a multitude of complex human problems would arise if the punishment is transferred to someone else.

It is argued by Christian theologians that such a transfer of punishment does not violate any principle of justice, because of the voluntary acceptance by the innocent person of the other person's punishment. What would you say in the case of a debtor, they ask, who is overloaded with debts beyond his capacity to pay and some God-fearing philanthropist decides to relieve him of his burden by paying his entire debt on his behalf? Our answer is that indeed we would loudly applaud such an act of immense generosity, kindness and sacrifice. But what would be the reaction of the person who confronts us with such a question, if the debt payable runs into trillions of pounds sterling and there steps forward a philanthropist who takes out a penny from his pocket, demanding that all that is due to the debtor should be cancelled out against that kindly penny offered as a substitute for that debt. What we have in the case of Jesus Christ[as] offering himself to be punished, for the sins of all humanity, is far more grotesquely disproportionate. Again, it is not only one debtor or all the debtors of one single generation, but we are talking about billions of born and unborn defaulters extending up to doomsday.

But that is not all. To conceive of crime through the example of a debtor owing money to someone else represents the most naive definition of sin that I have ever come across. This scenario which has been presented deserves to occupy our attention a little longer before we turn to some other aspects of crime and punishment.

Let us consider the case of a debtor called A, who owes a hundred thousand pounds to person B. If a rich philanthropist, in full command of his senses, seriously and genuinely wants to relieve the debtor of his burden, the common law would require him to pay to B all that person A owed him. But suppose the hypothetical philanthropist steps forward with the plea that person A should be absolved of his responsibility of payment to person B and instead he himself should be beaten up a little bit or imprisoned for three days and nights at the most, in A's place. If it really happened in real life it would be a treat to watch the horrified faces of the astounded judge and the confounded poor creditor B. But the philanthropist has yet to complete his plea for clemency. He would further stipulate: 'Oh, my lord that is not all I want in return for my sacrifice. I require all the debtors of the entire kingdom alive today, or to be born until the end of time to be absolved of their dues in return for my suffering of three days and nights'. At this point one's mind boggles.

How one wishes to propose to God, the Just God, that those who had been robbed of the fruits of their labour, or of the savings of their lives, should have been compensated to some degree at least! But the Christian God, it seems, is far kinder and more clement to the criminal than to the innocent who suffer at the hands of the criminal. It is a strange sense of justice indeed which results in the forgiveness of robbers, usurpers, the abusers of children, the torturers of the innocent and the perpetrators of all sorts of beastly crimes against humanity, provided that they believe in Jesus Christ[as] in their dying moments. What of the incalculable debt they owe to their tormented victims? Do a few moments of Jesus[as] in hell seem sufficient to purge them of their long lives of unpunished heinous guilt, which stretch for generation after generation?

Punishment Continues to be Meted Out

Let us now consider a different, more serious, category of crime, the consequences of which human nature simply cannot accept to be transferable. For instance, someone mercilessly abuses a child and even rapes and murders him or her. Human sensibilities would no doubt be violated to an unbearable degree. Suppose such a person continues to cause similar and greater suffering all around him without ever being caught and brought to justice. Having lived his life of crime unpunished by human hands, he closes in upon death but determines to elude even the greater punishment of the Judgement Day and suddenly decides, at last, to have faith in Jesus Christ[as] as his saviour. Would all his sins suddenly melt into nothingness and would he be left to glide into the other world free of sin like a newborn baby? Perhaps such a one who defers his belief in Jesus[as] till the time of death proves to be much wiser than the one who believes earlier in life. There always remained for the latter a danger of committing sins after belief and falling prey to the devil's designs and insinuations. Why not wait till death is close upon you, thereby giving the devil little chance and time to rob you of your faith in Jesus[as]? A free life of crime and pleasure, here on earth, and a rebirth in an eternal state of redemption is no mean bargain indeed.

Is this the wisdom of justice that the Christians attribute to God? Such a sense of justice, or such a God himself, is totally unacceptable to the human conscience, which He Himself created, without, alas, being able to discriminate right from wrong.

Looking at the same question in the light of human experience and human understanding, one has every right to denounce this philosophy to be meaningless and without foundation. It has no reality or substance. Human experience teaches us that it is always the prerogative of those who suffer at the hands of others to forgive or not to forgive. Sometimes governments, to celebrate a day of national rejoicing or for other reasons, may declare an amnesty to criminals without discrimination. But that does not in itself justify the act of pardoning those who have done some irreparable harm and caused perpetual suffering to their innocent fellow citizens. If the act of indiscriminate pardon at the hands of a government can by any measure be justified and if this is not considered by Christian theologians as a violation of the sense of justice then why do they not extend the same courtesy to God and concede to Him the right of forgiveness, as and when He so pleases? After all, He is the Supreme Sovereign, the Creator and Master of everything. If He pardons anyone for any crime that may have been committed against fellow beings, the Supreme Master has the unlimited power to compensate the aggrieved so generously as to make him perfectly satisfied with His decision. That being so where is the need for the sacrifice of His innocent

'Son'? This in itself constitutes a mockery of justice. We are born attuned to the attributes of God. He so declares in the Holy Bible:

> *Then God said, 'Let us make man in our image, after our likeness'.*
> *(Genesis 1:26)*

On the same subject in the Holy Quran He says:

$$ \ldots\ldots \text{فِطْرَتَ اللهِ الَّتِيْ فَطَرَ النَّاسَ عَلَيْهَا} \ldots\ldots $$

> *...And follow the nature made by Allah—the nature in which He*
> *has created mankind... (The Holy Quran 30:31)*

This tenet, common to Christian and Muslims alike, requires that human conscience be the best reflective mirror of God's conduct in a given situation. It is a matter of every day experience with us that many a time we forgive without having violated the sense of justice in the least. If we are wronged personally, then in respect of the crime committed against us we can go to any length in forgiveness. If a child hurts his parents by being disobedient or by causing damage to some precious household article, or by earning them a bad name, he has sinned against them. His parents may forgive him without their conscience pricking them or blaming them for having violated the sense of justice. But if their child destroys the property of their neighbour, or injures the child of another person, how could they decide to forgive the child for causing suffering to others? It would be deemed an act of injustice even according to their own consciences if they did so.

Crime and punishment have the same relationship as cause and effect, and they have to be proportionate to some degree. This aspect of the relationship between crime and punishment has already been discussed at some length with regards to financial misconduct of one man against another. The same argument applies with greater severity to other crimes like injuring, maiming or murdering innocent citizens or violating their honour in any manner. The greater the enormity of the crime, the more severe one would expect the nature and extent of punishment to be. If God can forgive all and sundry, as I do believe that He and only He can, then the question of Atonement in exchange for punishing an innocent person does not come into play at all. If, however, it is a question of the transference of one criminal's punishment to another innocent person who has opted for such a measure, then justice would most certainly demand that the punishment must be transferred in its entirety to the other person, without decreasing or diluting it to any degree. Again of that we have already said enough.

Do the Christians believe that this dictate of justice was applied in the case of Jesus[as], the 'Son' by 'God, the Father?' If so, it would mean that all the punishment due to all the criminals of the Christian world born at the time of Christ[as] or ever afterwards till Judgement Day was amassed, concentrated and brought to an infernal intensity of such a degree that the suffering of Jesus Christ[as] for merely three days and nights equalled the torture of all the punishment which the above mentioned sinners had earned or were to earn till that last day. If so, no Christian should ever be punished on earth by any Christian government. Otherwise, that would be tantamount to an act of gross injustice. All that the courts of law should do after reaching the verdict of guilty is to ask the Christian criminal to pray to Jesus[as] the 'Son' to save him. And the matter should rest and be brought to a close there and then. It would simply be a case of a book transfer of the criminal's account to that of Jesus Christ[as].

For the sake of illustration let us bring the United States of America into sharper focus and zoom in on the state of crime there. The crimes of mugging and murder are so widespread that it is difficult to keep a count of them. I remember once in New York, I tuned on a radio station which was devoted entirely to the reporting of capital crime. It was a most horrifying experience. It was so painful that half an hour was the maximum I could take it, no more. Almost every five minutes a new murder was committed in America and was reported, sometimes with grisly coverage by reporters who were actually witnessing the very murder in progress. It is not our intention to present a detailed picture of crime in America, but it is a matter of common knowledge that today America stands among the foremost in the list of countries where all sorts of crimes are rampant; particularly in larger cities such as Chicago, New York and Washington. In New York, mugging is commonplace, as is the maiming of innocent citizens who dare to resist it. This daily occurrence creates a most obnoxious picture of mutilation and murder for paltry gains.

Leaving aside, for the moment, the rising trend of crime throughout the world, in the case of America alone, one cannot fail to wonder about the relationship between the Christian concept of Sin and Atonement and the crimes committed daily. However much they may be removed from Christian values in their practice, at least this much goes to their credit that they do believe in the Christian doctrine of Sin and Redemption and also in Christ[as] as their saviour, but alas, to what avail. The majority of the criminals in America, of course, are so-called Christians. Though Muslims and others are no exception. Just because of all such criminals who belong to Christianity and believe in the reported voluntary sacrifice of Jesus Christ[as] for the sake of the believing sinners, will they all be pardoned by God? If so, in what way? Ultimately, a sizeable percentage from among them may get caught and get punished by the law of the land, but still a large number would either remain unapprehended or may only be punished for a part of the crimes which they may have committed over many years.

What would Christianity offer to those who are punished by law and what would it promise those who remain unapprehended here on earth? Will both be punished to varying degrees, or will they be punished indiscriminately?

Another dilemma relating to a criminal's redemption because of his belief in Jesus Christ[as] arises out of a less clear and undefined situation. If, for instance, a Christian commits a crime against an innocent non-Christian victim, he would be forgiven of course because of the blessings of his faith in Jesus[as]. The punishment of his crime will then be transferred to the account of Jesus[as] instead. But what would be the profit and loss statement of the poor innocent non-Christian victim? Poor Jesus[as] and the poor victim, both being punished for a crime they did not commit.

Our faculties are confounded if we try to imagine the enormity of all the crimes ever committed by humanity since the dawn of Christianity till the time when the sun of existence sets on human life. Have all these crimes been transferred to the account of Jesus Christ[as], peace and blessing of Allah be upon him? Have all these sins been accounted for in the small space of the three days and three nights that Jesus[as] is supposed to have suffered? Still one keeps on wondering, how could the vast sea of criminals so intensely embittered by the deadly poison of crime be sweetened and cleansed entirely of the effects of their crimes by the mere act of their believing in Jesus[as]. Again, one's thoughts are carried back to the remote past, when poor Adam and Eve so naively committed their first crime only because they were very cunningly duped and ensnared by Satan. Why was their sin not also washed clean? Did they not have faith in God? Was it a minor act of goodness to have faith in God the Father and was it their fault anyway that they had never been told of a 'Son' living eternally with God the Father? Why did not the 'Divine Son' take pity on them and beseech God the Father to punish him for their crimes instead? How one wishes that that had happened, since it might have been so much easier to be punished only for that one single faltering moment on the part of Adam and Eve. The entire story of humanity would certainly have been rewritten in the book of fate. A heavenly earth would have been created instead and Adam and Eve would not have been banished eternally from heaven along with the untold number of their unhappy progeny. Jesus[as] alone would have been banished from heaven merely for three days and three nights and that would have been that. Sadly, neither God the Father nor Jesus^{as} thought of this. Look how Jesus'^{as} holy, lovable reality is unfortunately transformed into a bizarre and unbelievable myth.

Justice and Forgiveness

The Christian philosophy of Crime and Punishment is not only utterly confusing for simple unprejudiced human intellect, but also raises many other relevant questions which are no less perplexing. The philosophy of relationship between justice and forgiveness, as maintained by the Christian philosophy of Atonement, attempts to explain why God Himself could not forgive. It is dependant entirely on an erroneous and arbitrary concept of justice, which takes it for granted that justice and forgiveness can never go hand in hand. That being so, why does the New Testament place so much emphasis on forgiveness when the question of human relationships is discussed? I have never read in any divine scriptures of any world religion a teaching that leans more one sidedly, and more overly emphasises the role of forgiveness. What a fantastic contrast with the traditional emphasis on justice found in Judaic teachings. An eye for an eye; a tooth for a tooth. That is justice—pure, simple and unattenuated. What a dramatic departure from this to the Christian teaching of turning the other cheek if slapped on one. Who gave the latter teaching which is against the earlier teachings of the Torah? Was the first teaching of the Torah, one is left wondering, a teaching by God the Father as against the diametrically opposed teaching of the New Testament, a teaching by Christ^{as} the 'Divine Son'? If so, why did the

'Divine Son' differ so drastically from his Father? Should such a conflict be taken as a genetical defect or an evolutionary change or was this Christian attitude of absolute forgiveness, as diametrically opposed to the Judaic emphasis on revenge, an example of a change on the part of God the Father? He seems to have dearly repented of what He had taught Moses[as] and the people of the Book and seems to have wanted very much to redress His own wrong.

As Muslims, we observe this fundamental shift in emphasis and see no contradiction because we believe in a God who combines in Him both the attributes of justice and forgiveness, without there being any inner conflict between the two attributes. We understand the transfer from Judaic teachings to those of Jesus Christ[as], not as a corrective measure of the original teachings but of their misapplication by the Jews. According to our belief, God is not only Just but is also Forgiving, Merciful and Beneficent. If He so desires, He does not stand in need of any outside help to forgive the sinful. But from the Christian point of view the problem acquires gigantic proportions. It appears that the God of the Torah was a God who knew only justice and had no sense of compassion or mercy. Apparently He was unable to forgive, however much He may have desired to do so. Lo, then came to His help 'God the Son' and extricated Him from His infernal dilemma. It seems that the 'Son' was 'All-Compassionate' as against the 'All-Vengefulness' of his Father. It is not just the apparent absurdity of this vision of the 'Son' which disturbs the human conscience. It also raises the question once again of the contradiction in their characters. Jesus[as] does not appear to be a true son of his Father, a genetic error again perhaps.

Another important area of inquiry is the attitude of other religions of the world towards sin and its consequences. Christianity is of course not the only religion to be a revealed religion. Numerically, non-Christians largely exceed Christians. Thousands of years of the known history of man, before Jesus Christ[as], saw many religions born and take root in different human soils in various parts of the world. Do these religions ever speak of a philosophy of forgiveness even remotely related to the Christian dogma of Atonement? What is their concept of God, or gods if they have now begun to believe in many? What is their concept of God's attitude towards sinful humanity?

Among the community of religions, the nearest to Christianity is perhaps Hinduism in this regard, but it is only partially so. Hindus also believe in an Absolute Just God, whose sense of justice demands that He must punish somehow every perpetrator of sin. But the resemblance ends there. No mention of a 'Divine Son' taking the entire consequences of the whole world of sinners upon his shoulders is even remotely indicated. On the contrary, we are told of an endless chain of crime and punishment in an endless number of reincarnations of the soul into animal flesh. Atonement only becomes accessible after the many times reincarnated soul has incurred punishment exactly the sum total of the crimes it committed during all its fateful experiences of reincarnation. To some it may sound weird and bizarre indeed, but there is certainly some inherent justice in this philosophy. There is a balance and symmetry in this view which is in perfect harmony with the concept of absolute justice.

Leaving aside Hinduism and other religions who advocate the philosophy of reincarnation with all its complexities of cause and effect, what is the role of forgiveness on the part of God in the remaining major or minor religions of the world? All such religions, and over a billion adherents of religions such as Hinduism, seem to be totally ignorant and uninformed of the myth of Atonement. This is very perplexing indeed. Who was in communion with mankind elsewhere in the history of religions? If it was not God the Father as in Christian doctrine, was the entire religious leadership of the world, except Jesus Christ[as], a pupil of the Devil himself? And where was God the Father? Why did He not come to the rescue when the rest of mankind was being led astray by the Devil in His name? Or were they, the rest of the humanity, a creation of a being other than the so-called God the Father? Again, why were they treated in such a step-fatherly way and abandoned to the cruel sway of the Devil?

Let us now turn our attention to this issue with reference to common human experience. It can be shown that forgiveness and justice are balanced and can coexist and do not always contradict each other. Sometimes justice demands that forgiveness must be extended, and sometimes it demands that forgiveness should be withheld. If a child is forgiven and is encouraged to commit more crime, then forgiveness is itself bordering on a crime and is against the sense of justice. If a criminal is forgiven, only to perpetrate more acts of crime and create suffering all around him because he is forgiven and encouraged, that would also be against the dictates of justice and would be tantamount to an act of cruelty to other innocent citizens. There are countless criminals of this type who are covered by the atonement of Jesus[as]. That in itself is contrary to justice. But if a child repents, for instance, and the mother is convinced that the same crime will not be repeated, then to punish the child would be counter to the sense of justice. When a repentant person suffers, that in itself is a punishment which may in some cases far exceed a punishment imposed from outside. People with a living conscience always suffer after committing a sin. As a consequence, the cumulative effect of the repeated pangs of conscience reaches a point where it may result in God taking pity on such a weak, oft-faltering, oft-repenting servant of His. This is the lesson in the relationship of justice to forgiveness, which people of high intellect and even people of ordinary understanding draw alike from a universal human experience. It is high time that Christians woke up from their dormant state of accepting Christian dogma without ever questioning its wisdom. If they re-examine Christian doctrine in the light of common sense and reasoning, they may still remain good practising Christians, but of a different and more realistic type. They would then believe even more, and with greater love and dedication in the human reality of Christ[as] as compared to the Christ[as] who is a mere figment of their imagination and no more real than fiction. The greatness of Jesus[as] lies not in his legend but in the supreme sacrifice of Jesus[as] the man and messenger. His was a sacrifice which moves the heart far more powerfully and profoundly than the myth of his death upon a cross and his revival from the dead after spending a few ghastly hours in hell.

Jesus Cannot Possibly Atone

Last but not least, how could Jesus[as] be born innocent when he had a human mother? If the sin of Adam and Eve had polluted the entire progeny of this unfortunate couple, then as a natural consequence, all male and female children must inherit the same genetic propensity to sin. Females were perhaps more likely to, because it was Eve who, as the instrument of Satan, enticed Adam. Therefore, the responsibility of sin falls squarely on the shoulders of Eve rather than of Adam. In the case of the birth of Christ[as], obviously it was a daughter of Eve who contributed the major share. The question that very forcefully arises is whether Jesus[as] inherited any gene bearing chromosomes from his human mother or not. If he did, then it was impossible for him to escape the inevitable inherited sin. If he did not inherit any chromosomes from his mother or from God the Father, then indeed his birth would be doubly miraculous. Only a miracle can produce a son who neither belongs to his father nor to his mother. What remains incomprehensible is why those chromosomes, provided by Eve, did not carry the innate tendency to sin to the child Jesus[as]. Suppose it happened somehow, and Jesus[as] had that innocence needed to carry the sins of mankind, on the condition that they believed in him and not otherwise, then another problem would arise: what happened, one may ask, to the progeny of Adam and Eve that died before the dawn of Christianity? How many billions of them might have got scattered throughout the world over five continents generation after generation. They must have lived and died without hope or even the possibility of ever hearing about the Christ[as] their Saviour who was not yet born. In fact, the entire humanity between Adam and Christ[as] seemed certainly to be doomed forever. Why were they never given even a remote chance to be forgiven? Would they be forgiven retrospectively, by Jesus Christ[as]? If so, why?

In other parts of the world, much larger by comparison to the tiny land of Judea, where people had never heard of Christianity even during the lifetime of Jesus Christ[as], what happens to them? They never did, nor ever could, believe in the 'Sonship' of Jesus Christ[as]. Will their sins go unpunished or will they be punished? If they go unpunished, for what reason? If they are punished, again by what logic? What chance did they have anyway? They were totally helpless. What a distorted sense of absolute justice!

Unwilling Sacrifice

Now let us turn to the act of Crucifixion itself. Here we are confronted with another insoluble dilemma. Jesus[as], as we are so insistently told, offered himself voluntarily to God the Father and was made the scapegoat for the sins of all humanity, provided, of course, they believed in him. But when the time of the acceptance of his wish approaches nigh and at last the glimmer of hope for sinful humanity is beginning to appear like the dawn of a new day, as we turn to Jesus[as] expecting to observe his joy, his happiness and his ecstasy at this most eventful moment of human history, how profoundly disappointed and manifestly disillusioned we are. Instead of finding a Jesus[as] impatiently awaiting the hour of jubilation what we see instead is a Jesus[as] weeping and crying and praying and beseeching God the Father to take away the bitter cup of death from him. He severely reproached one of his disciples when he caught him in the act of dozing off after spending such a fateful long day and suffering through a dark gloomy night which bade ill for him and his holy master. The Biblical account of this incident goes as follows:

> *Then Jesus went with them to a place called Gethsem'ane, and he said to his disciples, "Sit here, while I go yonder and pray." And taking with him Peter and the two sons of Zeb'edee, he began to be sorrowful and troubled. Then he said to them, "My soul is very sorrowful, even to death; remain here, and watch with me." And going a little farther he fell on his face and prayed, "My father, if it be possible, let this cup pass from me; nevertheless, not as I will, but as thou wilt." And he came to the disciples and found them sleeping; and he said to Peter, "So, could you not watch with me one hour? Watch and pray that you may not enter into temptation; the spirit indeed is willing, but the flesh is weak." Again, for the second time, he went away and prayed, "My Father, if this cannot pass unless I drink it, thy will be done." And again he came and found them sleeping, for their eyes were heavy. So, leaving them again, he went away and prayed for the third time, saying the same words.*
> *(Matt 26:36–44)*

Alas, as the Christian story unveils itself, the prayers and beseeching of neither Jesus[as] nor his disciples were accepted by God the Father and willy-nilly, despite his strong protestations, he was at last crucified. Was he the same person, the same prince of innocence and paragon of sacrifice who so bravely volunteered himself to take the burden of all of mankind's sins on his shoulders, or was it a different person? His conduct, both at the hour of the Crucifixion and during the Crucifixion itself, strongly casts shadow of doubt, either on the identity of Jesus Christ[as] or on the truth of the myth spun around his person. But of that later. Let us now return to our critical examination where we left it off.

Some other questions which arise from the last cry of agony by Jesus Christ[as] are as follows: Who uttered those deeply pathetic and touching words? Was it Jesus[as] the man or was it Jesus[as] the 'Son'?

If it was Jesus[as] the man who was abandoned, by whom he was abandoned and why? If we accept this option, it would also have to be taken for granted that till the last, Jesus[as] the man retained a single independent identity which could think and feel freely and individually. Did he die at the moment of the parting of the soul of Jesus[as] the 'Son of God' from the body of the man he had occupied? If so, why and how? If it was so and it was the body of the man which died after the soul of God deserted it, then the question would arise as to who got revived from the dead when the soul of God revisited the same body later on.

Again, this option would lead us to believe that it was not Jesus[as] the 'Son' who was suffering but the person of Jesus[as] the man who cried out in such agony and he was the one who suffered while Jesus[as] the 'Son' looked on in a state of total indifference and apathy. Then how can he justify the claim that it was he, the 'Son,' who suffered for the sake of humanity and not the man in him?

The other option is that we presume it was Jesus[as] the 'Son' who cried out, while the man in him, perhaps hopeful to begin a new life for himself, watched on in the uncertain expectation that along with the sacrifice of Jesus[as] the 'Son', he, Jesus[as] the man, whether he liked it or not, would also be slaughtered on the altar of his innocent cohabiter. What sense of justice ever motivated God to kill two birds with the same stone is perhaps another mystery.

If it was Jesus[as] the 'Son', and it was him indeed according to the general consensus of Christian churches, then the second question arising out of the answer of the first would be about the identity of the second party involved in that monologue of Jesus[as] (Matt 26:39,42). We have two options open to us:

One, that the 'Son' was addressing the Father, complaining that he was abandoned in the hour of need. This inescapably leads us to believe that they were two different persons who did not coexist in a single mutually merged personality, equally sharing all attributes and putting them into play simultaneously with equal share. One appears to be the supreme arbiter, the all powerful possessor of the ultimate faculty of taking decisions. The other, the poor 'Son,' seems to be entirely deprived or maybe temporarily dispossessed of all the domineering characters which his Father enjoys. The central point which must be kept in focus is the fact that their opposite wills and wishes nowhere seem more at odds and at variance with each other than they do during the last act of the Crucifixion drama.

The second question is, would these two distinct persons, with individual thoughts, individual values and individual capacities, feel pain and agony if they were 'two in one' and 'one in two?' So another question would require many a long dialogue between theologians regarding the possibility of God being able to suffer pain and punishment. Even if He were able to do so, only half of God would suffer while the other half would be incapable of doing so either by design or by the compulsion of His nature.

As we proceed further in the shadowy world of this twisted philosophy, light begins to get dimmer and dimmer and we find confusion heaped upon confusion. Another problem is, whom was Christ[as] addressing if he was God himself? When he addressed his father, he himself was an inseparable part of the Father, so we are told. So what was he saying and to whom? This question must be answered with a free conscience, without resorting to dogma. It becomes a dogma only when it cannot be explained in human terms. According to the Biblical statement, when Jesus[as] was about to give up the ghost, he cried addressing God the Father: "why hast thou forsaken me?" (Matt 27:46) Who had forsaken whom? Had God forsaken God?

Who Was Sacrificed?

The other problem we have to take note of is that the man in Jesus[as] was not punished, nor by any logic should he have been punished, because he had never opted to carry the load of humanity's sin. This new element, entering into the debate, leads us to a very peculiar situation which we have not considered before. One is compelled to wonder about the relationship of the man in Jesus[as] with the inherited propensity to commit sin, common to all the progeny of Adam and Eve. At best one can bring oneself to believe that in the duality of the 'Divine Son' and the man occupying the same body, it was only the 'Divine Son' who was innocent. But what about the man living alongside him? Was he also born out of genes and character provided by God? If so, then he should behave like the divine in Jesus[as] and no excuse would be acceptable if he went remiss in this or that, with the plea that he only did so because he was a man. If there was nothing of God in him, that is, in the man in Jesus[as], then we must concede that he was simply an ordinary human being, perhaps half a human being. Yet that human person, amalgamated with Jesus[as], has to be human enough to inherit the disposition to sin. If not, why not?

Obviously there is no gain in saying that being a man distinctly separate from his divine partner, he must have sinned independently with the entire responsibility of sin upon his human shoulders. This scenario will not be complete without presenting Jesus[as] the 'Son of God' dying, not so unselfishly after all, for the sake of humanity, but his prime concern might have been for his half brother, the man in him.

All this is extremely difficult, if not impossible, to digest intellectually. But our point of view presents no such problems. It was the innocent person Jesus[as] the man, without there being any duality in him, who uttered this cry of astonishment and agony.

The Dilemma of Jesus

Let me once again make it clear that I do not disbelieve in Jesus[as] but have profound respect for him as a messenger of God with exceptional sacrifices to his credit. I understand Jesus[as] to be a holy man, going through a period of great trial. But as the narration of the act of Crucifixion begins to unfold and comes to a close we are left with no choice but to believe that Jesus[as] did not volunteer himself for death upon the cross. The night before the day his enemies attempted to murder him by crucifixion we hear him praying all night, along with his disciples, because the truth of his claim was at stake. It is said in the Old Testament that an impostor, who attributes things to God which He had never said, would hang on a tree and die upon it an accursed death.

But the prophet who presumes to speak a word in my name which I have not commanded him to speak, or who speaks in the name of other gods, that same prophet shall die. (Deuteronomy 18:20)

And if a man has committed a crime punishable by death and he is put to death, and you hang him on a tree, his body shall not remain all night upon the tree, but you shall bury him the same day, for a hanged man is accursed by God;... (Deuteronomy 21:22–23)

Jesus[as] knew that if this happened, the Jews would celebrate with ecstasy and proclaim him to be an impostor whose falsehood had finally been proved beyond a shadow of doubt on the authority of the Divine Scriptures. This was the reason why he was so anxious to escape the bitter cup of death; not out of cowardice, but out of fear that his people would be misled and would fail to recognise his truth if he died upon the cross. All night he prayed so piteously and helplessly that to read the account of his agony and misery is heart rending. But as this real life drama proceeds to a close, the climax of his emotional distress, dejection and hope-lessness is fully displayed in his last cry: *"Eli, Eli, la'ma sabach-tha'ni?"* that is, "My God, my God, why hast thou forsaken me?" (Matt 27:46)

One must notice that it was not agony alone expressed in that cry but obviously there was mingled with it an element of sur-prise, bordering on horror.

After he was brought back to consciousness, with the help of some of his dedicated disciples who applied to his wounds an ointment they had prepared before Crucifixion and which con-tained all the ingredients needed for mitigating pain and healing wounds, he must have been so wonderfully and happily surprised and his faith in a loving true God would have been reinstated and revitalised in a manner seldom experienced by man in its intensity and boundlessness.

The fact that the ointment had been prepared in advance con-stitutes a strong proof that Jesus'[as] disciples were indeed expecting him to be delivered from the cross alive, very much in need of medicinal treatment.

From the above, it becomes comfortingly clear that the con-cepts of Inherited Sin and of Crucifixion are based only on the conjecture and wishful thinking of Christian theologians at a later date. It is quite likely that they were born out of some pre-Christian myths of a similar nature, which, when applied to the circumstances of Jesus Christ[as], tempted them to read close simi-larities between the two and create a similar myth. However, whatever the mystery or paradox, as we see it, there is no evi-dence whatsoever that the Christian philosophy of Sin and

Atonement was based on anything which Jesus[as] might have said or done or taught. He could never have preached anything so contrary, and so diametrically opposed, to human intellect.

Did God the Father Suffer as Well?

Coming to the nature of the 'Son', we cannot believe that he was thrown into Hell Fire, as that would mean an internal contradiction with himself. Returning to the basic concept of Christianity we see that it is said that God and the 'Son' are two persons but of the same nature and substance. It is impossible for one to go through an experience while the other does not share in it. How can we believe that one aspect of God, the 'Son', was being tormented, while God the Father remained unscathed? If He did not suffer, it would be tantamount to breaking the Unity of God. Three persons in one becomes even more inconceivable because the experiences of each constituent of Trinity have turned out to be so different and remote from each other that it appears impossible for one God to be in the raging fire of hell, and at the same time the other to remain perfectly aloof and untouched. There is no other choice for the Christians of today but either to sacrifice the Unity of God and believe in three different Gods, like the pagans of pre-Christianity such as the Romans and the Greeks, or to remain true to themselves and believe that God is one and as such, two aspects of God cannot undergo contradictory states. When a child suffers, it is impossible for the mother to remain calm and peaceful. She must suffer as well, sometimes more than the child. What was happening to God the Father when He made

His 'Son' suffer the agony of three days in hell? What was happening to God the 'Son'? Was he divided into two persons, with two forms and substances? One form suffering in hell and the other completely outside, not suffering at all? If God the Father was suffering then what was the need of creating the Son, when He himself could have suffered? So this is a very direct question. Why did He not just suffer Himself? Why draw out such a difficult plan to resolve the problem of forgiveness?

The Punishment of Fire

Here, the question of hell to which, according to the Christian doctrine, Jesus[as] was confined, should be examined more closely. What sort of hell was it, Was it the same hell we read about in the New Testament, which says:

> "*The Son of man will send his angels, and they will gather out of his kingdom all causes of sin and all evildoers, and throw them into the furnace of fire; there men will weep and gnash their teeth.*"
> (*Matt 13:41–42*)

Before we proceed further, it has to be very clearly understood what the New Testament means by the punishment of fire or the punishment of hell. Is it a fire which burns the soul, or is it a carnal fire which consumes the body and thereby tortures the soul? Do the Christians believe that after death we will return to the same body which the soul left behind to disintegrate to earth and ashes, or will there be a new body created for each soul and will the resurrected person experience a sort of reincarnation?

If it is carnal fire and a corporeal punishment, then one has to extend one's imagination to the limit of its tethers to imagine what may have happened in the case of Jesus Christ[as]. Before being subjected to the Fire, was his soul re-imprisoned in the body of the man he had been haunting all his life on earth, or was he somehow relegated to an astral body? If the latter is the case then that astral body would have been beyond the reach of the carnal fire of hell to scorch, punish or destroy. On the other hand if we accept the scenario that the body of the man he had occupied would be reconstructed for Jesus[as] as a sort of medium through which he could suffer hell, then one cannot fail to notice another blow done to the principle of divine justice. Poor man, first of all he was practically hijacked for all his life by an alien soul, but then as a reward for the hospitality forced upon him he would burn in hell for no crime of his own. The credit of his sacrifice being totally monopolised by the alien occupant within him. Again, what about the soul of that man? Perhaps he did not have a soul of his own. If he did not, then the man in Jesus[as] and the God in Jesus[as] had to be one and the same person and the plea that Jesus[as] acted sometimes by his human impulses and sometimes by Divine Will is reduced to sheer hocus-pocus. The only formula acceptable to any intellect is that one soul and one body equals one person. Two souls and one body is a bizarre idea which can only be entertained by those who believe in people being haunted by ghosts or similar things.

Sacrifice and Spiritual Bliss

If the second option is more acceptable to the Christian Theologians in that it assumes only the soul of Jesus[as] to have entered hell and that hell to be a spiritual hell, then there seems to be no reason why we should reject this suggestion as nonsensical. However, spiritual hell is only created by pangs of conscience or a sense of guilt. In the case of Jesus Christ[as] neither was applicable. When you accept the penalty of another's crime, being innocent yourself, it is not pangs of conscience which are generated but quite the opposite. The soul of such a person should vibrate with a sense of nobility and self-sacrifice, which would be tantamount to spiritual heaven rather than hell.

Now we turn to the question of the body that was occupied by Jesus[as], and the meaning of death in relation to that body and also to the meaning of revival in the same context. To the best of our knowledge the body of Jesus Christ[as] had to be an integral part of the 'Sonship' of Jesus[as]. Otherwise, he would have no common meeting ground left to him for his divinity and humanity to merge upon and play distinctly different roles under certain conditions. At times we should see the man taking charge of affairs, provided he had a separate soul himself, and at times we should observe the Divine asserting Himself and controlling the man's faculties of head and heart. Again we emphasise that this can happen only if there are two distinct personalities locked up in a single being.

Meaning of Death in Relation to Christ

Having clearly understood the different options regarding the relative roles that the Divine and the Man in Jesus^{as} could have played, we try to comprehend the application of the word 'death' and its full meaning in relation to him.

If he died for three days and nights, then death has to be understood in terms of the soul having been severed from the body, and the soul departing. This means that the soul must depart the body and break off its relationship so completely that only a very dead corpse is left behind. So far so good. Jesus^{as} was at last relieved of his imprisonment in the carnal body of a man. However, liberation from this imprisonment should not be considered a punishment at all. The return of the divine soul of the 'Son' to the same sublime state of existence cannot be treated in any way like ordinary human death. Human death is fearsome not because the soul leaves the body and severs its ties by gaining a new consciousness, but the horrors of death are mainly on account of one's permanently severing ties with many dear ones left here on earth, and leaving behind one's possessions and different objects of love. Many a time it so happens that a man who has nothing to live for, prefers to die rather than live an empty life.

In the case of Jesus^{as}, the feeling of remorse could not have been present. For him the window of death was open only in one single direction, that of gain and not of loss. Why should his departure from the body be considered an extremely pitiable and agonizing experience? Again, if he died once and literally, not metaphorically gave up the ghost, as the Christians would have us believe, then returning to the same body is the most unwise step attributed to him. Was he reborn when he returned to the body that he had abandoned during the hour of death? If this process is only to be described as the revival or resurrection of Jesus[as], then the body should also have been eternalized. But what we read in the Bible is a completely different story. According to that story Jesus[as] was resurrected from the dead by entering the same body in which he had been crucified and that was called his regaining of life. That being so, what would be the meaning of the act of his abandoning the body once again? Would that not be tantamount to a second death?

If the first departure from the body was death, then most certainly the second time he is considered to have abandoned the human body, he should be declared eternally dead. When the soul abandons the body first time, you call it death; when it returns to the same body, you call it life after death. But what would you call it when the soul leaves the same body once again never to return—will it be called eternal death or eternal life according to the Christian jargon? It has to be eternal death and nothing more. Contradiction upon contradiction, a very nerve racking experience indeed!

If it is suggested that the body was not abandoned the second time, then we have a strange scenario in which God the Father exists as an infinite incorporeal spiritual being while the 'Son' remains trapped in the restricted confines of mortal existence.

Limited Suffering for Unlimited Sin

It may be suggested that it is not always the pangs of conscience which create a miserable state of mind and heart in those who are sensitive to their faults. On the other hand, intense sympathy for the sufferings of others may also create a life of agony for someone who is totally or partially innocent of crime, but has that sublime spiritual quality of suffering for the sake of others. That would also create a similitude of hell. Mothers suffer for their ailing babies. The human experience stands witness to the fact that sometimes for a permanently disabled child the entire life of the mother is turned into a living hell. So why cannot we concede to Jesus[as] that noble quality of being able to suffer for the sake of others? Why not indeed! But why only three days and nights? Why not for his entire sojourn on earth, and even before and after that? Noble people do not suffer only temporarily for a very limited period of hours or days. Their hearts do not rest in peace unless they see misery mitigated or alleviated entirely. The hell which we are considering is not the prerogative of an innocent divine person only; it is a noble quality shared to some degree even by the beasts of the jungle for their near ones.

After a few more remarks I shall rest my case, but I have one other important issue to briefly touch upon. The punishment prescribed by God for Jesus Christ[as] only lasted for three days and three nights, while the sinners for whom he was punished, had committed sins so horrible and for so long that, according to the Bible, their punishment was to be eternal suffering in hell. So what sort of a just God was it that when it came to the punishment of those created by Him, people who were not His sons or daughters, they were to be punished eternally? But when it came to the punishment of His own 'Son', for sins he had voluntarily taken upon himself, suddenly the punishment was reduced to only three days and three nights. No comparison whatsoever. If this is justice then let justice not be. How would God look at the conduct of human beings, whom He has Himself created with His right hand, if they dispense justice as they learnt it from Him by applying different measures to their own children, and very different to those of others? Will God the Father watch this loyal imitation with ecstasy or horror? This is very difficult indeed to answer.

What did Atonement Change?

As far as the effect of the crucifixion of Jesus Christ[as] in relation to the punishment of sin is concerned, we have already established that faith in Jesus Christ[as] has in no way reduced the punishment of sin, prescribed by God, for Adam and Eve and their progeny. All human mothers still bear their children with the pains of labour, and it is still with labour that man earns his bread. We can consider this from another angle, that of a broad comparison between the Christian and non-Christian world since the time of Jesus Christ[as]. No believers in Christ[as] can show a remarkable change, in any period of history, of their women delivering their children without pains, and their men earning their bread without labour. They do not show any difference in this regard in comparison to the non-Christian world.

As far as the disposition to commit sins is concerned, the world of believers in Christ[as] compared with the world of non-believers does not record any evidence that the disposition to commit sin is totally obliterated among the category of believers in Christ[as].

In addition to this, one may indeed wonder why having faith in God is considered so inferior to having faith in His 'Son'. This is especially relevant to the time before this tightly kept, age-old secret (that God had a 'Son') was disclosed to mankind. Of course there were people who had faith in God and His Unity.

Also innumerable people were born since Christ[as] in every religion and land of the earth who believed in God and His oneness. Why did faith in God not bear any influence on human crime and punishment? Again why could not God the Father display that nobility of suffering for the sake of sinners which His nobler 'Son' displayed? Most certainly the Son seems to possess higher moral values (God forbid) than his less civilised Father. Is Divinity evolving and still in the process of attaining perfection, one may ask?

CHAPTER THREE

THE ROLE OF THE HOLY GHOST

SO FAR, WE HAVE DISCUSSED THE QUESTION of Jesus[as] the so-called 'Son' and also God the supposed literal 'Father' of Jesus[as]. Yet there is a third person by the name of the 'Holy Ghost' who, according to Christian dogma, despite having a distinct individual personality, is still amalgamated and so completely and eternally fused with the 'Father' and the 'Son' that their merger creates singleness in three. Now we turn our attention to this question by enquiring whether the Holy Ghost has an ego separate from God or Jesus[as], or do they share one single ego? Ego can be described here as the ultimate seat of consciousness which, in the final analysis, is indivisible and specific to each individual. The same ultimate awareness of one's being as distinct from that of others gives birth to 'I', and 'my' and 'mine', as against 'he' and 'his' and 'you' and 'yours'.

Bringing into focus the three parts of Divinity, we must resolve whether the three have distinct egos of their own or not. If they do not have distinct separate egos, then to attribute to them personages would become inconceivable. Each person, however close he may be to another, has to enjoy a separate individual consciousness of his being.

The 'official position' of most churches is very clear and well defined, claiming that each of the three entities of God's personage had a distinctly separate personage 'of its' own. So it is not just 'Three in One', but rather it is three persons in one person. The bitter encounter of Jesus[as] with death and all its fateful consequences must have been equally shared by the Holy Ghost. So also, he should have been included in the sacrifice along with Jesus[as]. Again, he must have suffered hell in the company of Jesus[as] and God the Father. If not, then one cannot escape drawing the inevitable conclusion that not only were they three distinct and different persons, but also their emotions and faculties relating to head and heart must have been different, separate and insulated from those of each other.

In trying to take further our vision of the Trinity we should attempt to visualize the fact of three persons merging together, or existing as merged together eternally as one. So far we have failed to see how they could have merged in their emotions and thought processes.

The only option left, therefore, is a merger in the body. It reminds us on a different scale of a hydra-headed monster, mentioned in the Greek mythology, which possessed many heads that grew again when cut off. Of course, man cannot understand the true nature of God and how His attributes function, but it is very easy and simple to believe in one single entity without specific areas to which certain functions are attributed and confined, like head, heart and kidneys etc. But the scenario of separate individual thoughts and feelings is certainly at variance with the aforementioned scenario of a single entity. It creates an image of God which is very difficult to believe and conceive for human beings, many of whom have lived long with Christian dogma without questioning it, and have somehow shut their eyes to such glaring violations against the human intellect, which was supposedly created by God himself.

The Holy Ghost and Creation

We do not observe any role played by the Holy Ghost or Jesus Christ[as] in the divine plan of creation: In the beginning God created the heavens and the earth (Genesis 1:1). Obviously it is 'God the Father' who is referred to in the Old Testament without any hint of a reference to Christ[as] or the Holy Ghost In the entire pre-Christian era, among all the Jews who believed in the Old Testament and must have heard this verse hundreds of thousands of times, there was not one who could read the name of Christ[as] or that of the Holy Ghost in the story of the creation of the Universe. In his Gospel, St John suggests 'Word' to stand for Jesus[as] (John 1:1)[*]. It is strange that such an important subject has been taken up by the author of only one Gospel; by someone who was not even a disciple of Jesus[as]. Even if one accepts his word to be the word of God, still it can only be understood to mean the Will of God; this is a concept that is common to many religions with reference to Creation.

---

[*] In the beginning was the Word, and the Word was with God, and the Word was God. (John 1:1)

Surprisingly, the secret of Christ's[as] and the Holy Ghost's participation in the Creation remained a secret to Jesus[as] himself. We read not a single statement of Jesus Christ[as] in which he claims to be the 'Word'. Therefore, neither Jesus[as] nor the Holy Ghost had any part to play in the shaping and making of Creation. Again it was God the Father alone, we are told, who fashioned man from dust with His own hands. I have never read anywhere in any Christian writings that the two hands belonged to Jesus[as] and the Holy Ghost Hence God created everything without the slightest help from, or participation of, Jesus[as] or the Holy Ghost Were they passive observers generally in agreement with what God was doing or did they actually participate? If the latter is more acceptable to Christian theologians then immediately the question arises whether each of them was individually capable of creating, without the help of the others, or were they only capable in their totality? And again, if all three were essentially needed to pool their functions together to create, then was their share equal, or did one have a larger share of the labour put into the process of creation? Were they three persons with different powers both in intensity and kind, or did they share their powers equally? One has to admit that whichever of the two options is taken, each of the components of Trinity becomes incompetent to create anything by itself.

If the same argument is extended to other Divine functions, the same question will continue to plague the Christian theologians. At the end of the day Christians will have to admit that they do not believe in one simple entity of God, with three aspects and expressions of one single central power and majesty. But rather that they believe in three complementary components of God-head that are three segments of the body of God. The question of being equal or unequal would then be assigned a relatively minor status.

Take, for instance, the attribute of Justice and Forgiveness. The 'Son' appears to be more compassionate whereas God the Father appears to be less just than the Holy Ghost, who took no part in the injustice on the part of God the Father.

The second possibility we mentioned was that Jesus[as] and the Holy Ghost played an inert role in the processes of creation and the government of the laws of nature. That being so, it raises many more questions. First of all, what is the assigned role of the two partners of God in the discharging of their Divine functions? If they are passive, silent observers, like sleeping partners, then they are automatically relegated to a secondary, inferior position where they coexist with God but without, in practicality, sharing His Powers. This concept of God having two non-functional appendices is very bizarre, to say the least I wonder whose conscience it can satisfy. Rationally it is, of course, unacceptable and does not harmonize with the Christian concept of 'Three in One' and 'One in Three'. The oneness in three cannot be reached, or even remotely conceived of, without there being a total merger of will, of powers and of whatever experience of life that can be attributed to a single living entity.

In the case of Holy Ghost, being a separate person, unless that person merges completely and irrevocably, losing all its identity in the other two, there remains no future hope of the emergence of a hydra-headed god with single thoughts, a single will and a single body.

Mystery or Paradox

It is acceptable for a person to believe in something not fully understandable to him because of some irrefutable evidence in its favour. For example, many people do not understand the phenomena which collectively make it possible to create radio transmission and receptor sets, and also the transmission of electrical audio-video pulses that are converted into televised pictures and sound. Yet even the most unlettered person would have to believe in the reality of radio and television. Similarly, most of us do not understand how computers work, yet very few in this contemporary age would dare to deny the existence of computers simply for this reason. Such cases may be classified as mysteries, but there is no question of denying their existence or deriding those who believe in them, provided of course, that they are fully backed up and supported by irrefutable evidence.

We also accept that a much more lenient attitude can be, and is exercised, regarding many mysteries which exist in the form of religious dogmas. A very large number of human beings believe in such dogmas without being able to understand or to explain them. They seem to inherit such doctrines through generations and acquire a taken-for-granted attitude towards them. But when the elements of contradiction and paradox find their way into religious dogmas, no excuse in their favour can be accepted on the plea that belief in perplexing mysteries also provides justifica-

tion for believing in paradoxes. It is here that the problem becomes complicated. I can believe in something that I do not
understand, but I cannot believe in something that is contradictory in itself, nor I hope, can any other person in his senses. For
instance, I cannot understand how a watch is made; that is alright,
but I have no right to believe that a watch is simultaneously a live
barking and kicking dog. This is not a mysterious dogma, but
simply a glaring contradiction.

When there is any contradiction between two or more attributes of God, or when there are inconsistencies between the word
of God and the act of God, then the limits of mystery are trans-
gressed by a large margin and one finds oneself drifting out of the
sphere of mystery and into a world of fantasy. When so proved, it
is but natural to expect that the believers in contradictions should
make amends in their beliefs and accordingly effect a reform in
their faith. Unfortunately, however, in our dialogues with some
Christian ministers we find them tenaciously holding the view
that belief in Jesus[as] as a god and simultaneously as a man is not
contradictory. Nor does it appear contradictory to them that one
person can be three persons simultaneously without there being
the slightest difference in their character. They insist that to
believe in one God and also to believe in a three pronged godhead, composed of God, the Holy Ghost and the Son, is not a
paradox but simply a mystery.

They shut their eyes to the contradictions in their claim that
God remains a single entity despite the fact that the person of
God, 'The Father,' is distinctly different from the person of Jesus[as],
the 'Son', and the 'Holy Ghost'. When we point out to them, in

amazement, that we are talking of three persons, and not about the different aspects, moods and attributes of a single person, and that God being 'One in Three' and 'Three in One' is certainly not a mystery but a glaring contradiction, they nod their heads in sympathy with us and politely ask us to step into contradictions operating in another area of discussion. They require us to first believe in the unbelievable and then to progress from there, to develop a faith in contradictions, or mysteries as they would much rather call them. A non-Christian therefore cannot understand the contradictions of Christian dogmas and to understand what he cannot believe in, he must believe without understanding. This is the world of Christian fantasy into which we, non-Christians, are advised to enter. But this magic flying carpet of fantasy refuses to take flight if a non-believer steps onto it.

CHAPTER FOUR

CRUCIFIXION

BEFORE TURNING TO THE BIBLICAL DESCRIPTION of events relating to Christ[as] and his crucifixion, perhaps it would not be out of place to mention here, in brief, the Aḥmadiyya Muslim understanding of what happened during and after the crucifixion of Jesus Christ[as]. This issue will be briefly touched upon here and a detailed discussion will follow later.

We believe that the crucifixion of Jesus[as] was an attempt made on his life, like any attempted murder. Crucifixion was only the weapon used in that murderous attempt. However, the attempt to crucify him failed in inflicting death. This is tantamount to saying that they failed to crucify him. When we say this, we express ourselves exactly as we would in any other case of attempted murder. If an attempt is made on someone's life and the attempt fails, it cannot be said that the intended victim was murdered. For instance, if such an attempt is made with a sword, and the attempt fails, no one can say that the intended victim was put to the sword. So we believe, as Muslims, that only an attempt to murder Jesus[as] was made: crucifixion being the instrument of the attempted murder. After a few hours of intense suffering upon the cross, before death could overtake him, he was taken down from the cross in a state of deep coma from which he was revived later on. As no state can permit a person who is condemned to death legal cover and protection if he somehow escapes execution, so also under the Roman law, no immunity could be extended to Jesus[as] beyond the point of his crucifixion. That provided Jesus[as] with enough cause to escape from the Roman territory to a land of freedom. But he also had to perform a commission and had a prophecy to fulfil. There were those lost sheep of Israel, who after their exodus under the Babylonian and Roman invasion, scattered in many eastern lands and were awaiting his ministry. This was the other very strong reason for Jesus[as] to have immigrated from the land of Judea to those foreign lands where the Jews had settled over a period of many centuries. This much should suffice for the time being.

I want to make one thing clear to those who demand from us a proof of the natural death of Jesus Christ[as] after he was saved from the cross. They are shifting the burden of proof on us without justification. There are natural phenomena known to man which are universally understood. We know that the life span of man on earth does not extend beyond a hundred and fifty years or so; certainly it is not a thousand years or more. This is a common experience relating to the span of human life on earth. If someone thinks that something contradictory to this rule has happened, then the burden of proof falls on his shoulders, not on someone who believes in the rule rather than the exception. This should be applied to the situation enveloping the life and death of Jesus Christ[as]. Those who believe that he did not die must provide the proof. But those who claim that he must have died, only follow the laws of nature and should not be required to prove it beyond that. Otherwise, anyone could say that his great great great... grandfather has not died. If such a claimant goes around challenging everyone to prove otherwise, what would be their reaction? How can a poor listener meet such a challenge? He can only point out that the laws of nature operate on every human being and spare no one. So if someone is making claims against the laws of nature, the onus of proof is on him. This is the first answer. But I will now make another humble attempt to try to make things clearer from a different viewpoint. Whatever his relationship with God, was it beyond Jesus Christ[as] to die? The Christians them-selves believe that he died. If it was against his nature to die, this could not have happened in the first place. Yet we all agree that he died at least once. The remaining part of the enquiry would be as to when he died. Was it on the cross or was it afterwards.

The Sign of Jonah

We can prove from the Bible that God did not abandon him and saved him from the ignoble death upon the cross. This can be studied in the light of the facts relating to the period before the Crucifixion, as well as the facts of the Crucifixion itself and after it, as related by the New Testament.

Long before the Crucifixion, Jesus[as] promised that no sign would be shown to the people other than the sign of Jonah[as].

Then some of the scribes and Pharisees said to him, "Teacher, we wish to see a sign from you." But he answered them, "An evil and adulterous generation seeks for a sign; but no sign shall be given to it except the sign of the prophet Jonah. For as Jonah was three days and three nights in the belly of the whale, so will the Son of man be three days and three nights in the heart of the earth. The men of Nin'eveh will arise at the judgment with this generation and condemn it; for they repented at the preaching of Jonah, and behold, something greater than Jonah is here." (Matt 12:38–41)

So before we determine what happened to Jesus[as], we must understand what happened to Jonah[as], because Jesus[as] claimed that the same miracle would be repeated. What was the Sign of Jonah[as]? Did he die in the belly of the fish, and was he later on revived from death? There is unanimity among all Christian, Jewish and Muslim scholars that Jonah[as] did not die in the belly of the fish. He precariously hung between life and death and was miraculously saved from that situation, while any other person in his place would have died. Yet some subtle laws of nature, under the Divine command, must have conspired together to save him from death. Remember, we are not debating the issue of that being possible or not. We are only pointing out that Jesus[as], when he said that the like of what happened to Jonah[as] would also happen to him, could only have meant that what everyone understood to have occurred in the case of Jonah[as] would occur in his own case. No one in the entire world of Judaism, whether in the land of Judea or anywhere else the Jews had dispersed and settled, would have received a different message from this claim of

Jesus[as]. They all believed that Jonah[as], miraculously or otherwise, survived for three days and nights in the belly of the fish and did not die in that period for a single moment. Of course, we have our own reservations regarding this view. The story of Jonah[as] as told to us in the Holy Quran does not mention anywhere that it was for three days and nights that Jonah[as] suffered his trials in the belly of the fish. However, we return to the case in point and try to bring to light the actual similarities which were predicted by Jesus Christ[as] between Jonah[as] and himself. Those similarities spoke clearly of spending three days and nights in extremely precarious circumstances and of a miraculous revival from near death, and not of coming back to life from the dead. The same, Jesus[as] claimed, would happen in his case.

Jesus' Promise to the House of Israel

The second important piece of evidence is that Jesus[as] told his people that the sheep of the House of Israel who dwelt in and around Judea were not the only sheep, and that he was sent by God not only to them but also to the other sheep of the same flock. Just as he had come to retrieve them he would also go and retrieve the others as well.

> *And I have other sheep, that are not of this fold; I must bring them also, and they will heed my voice. So there shall be one flock, one shepherd. (John 10:16)*

Now according to common knowledge, between the time of his promise and Crucifixion, he never left the land of Judea for anywhere else. The question is, if Jesus[as] ascended to heaven eternally, had the lost sheep of Israel also ascended earlier? The Christians believe that after having been taken down from the cross as dead, his soul returned to his body after three days or so and then he was seen climbing into the clouds and disappearing into the unknown recesses of the heavens, only to reach ultimately the throne of his Father and to sit on His right hand eternally from then on. If this is true then we will be faced with a very grave dilemma indeed. We shall have to choose between two positions, one taken by Jesus[as] himself and the other by his followers. The two positions are so uncompromising that accepting one would certainly negate the other. If Jesus[as] was right, as we believe he was, then before ascending to the heaven he should have remembered his own promise and sought some more time from 'God the Father' to tarry a bit longer on earth so that he could go to the countries where many of the Israeli tribes before him had gone and settled. He could not have ascended to the heavens without breaking his promise and trust, blemishing and irreparably damaging his perfect god, perfect man image. If, on the contrary, the Christian theologians are to be considered right and it is accepted that Jesus[as] actually forgot his commitment to the house of Israel and left straight for the heavens, then we must conclude with a heavy heart that the Christian theologians are right indeed but, alas, Christianity turns out to be false. Because if Jesus[as] is proved to be false, Christianity cannot be true.

We believe that he was a true Prophet of God and could not have made a false promise. What he meant by the lost sheep was the ten tribes of Israel, who had earlier migrated from Judea and had gone to remote eastern lands. His promise, therefore, was that he would not be killed on the cross but would be given a long life to pursue his mission and that he was a Prophet not just for the two Israeli tribes living around him, but for all the Israelites. Together, the above two pieces of evidence provide the positive indication of what was to happen to Jesus Christ[as] after the Crucifixion.

Events of the Crucifixion

Another point relevant to this issue relates to the fixing of the date and time by Pilate for carrying out the Crucifixion. Even before he fixed the date and time we read of other things which, one should not be surprised to believe, might have played an important role regarding his final decision. First of all we know on the authority of the New Testament that Pilate's wife was strongly averse to her husband passing judgement against Jesus[as] because of the influence of a dream she had the night before the trial of Jesus[as]. (Matt 27:19)

She was so terrified by the effect of the dream, which led her to believe that Jesus[as] was absolutely innocent, that she thought it imperative to disturb the court proceedings to convey the message of the dream to her husband. Perhaps it was this urgent protestation by his wife that led Pilate to make a show of absolving himself of the responsibility of his condemnation of Jesus[as]:

So when Pilate saw that he was gaining nothing, but rather that a riot was beginning, he took water and washed his hands before the

crowd, saying, "I am innocent of this man's blood; see to it
yourselves." (Matt 27:24)

This amounted to a confession on his part that
Jesus[as] was indeed innocent and that the harsh judgement passed
by him was under duress. It is quite clear from the New Testament that the powerful Jewish community had colluded against
Jesus[as] and was determined to have him punished. So any decision
by Pilate contrary to Jewish wishes could have resulted in a grave
law and order situation. This was Pilate's compulsion which
rendered him helpless and was displayed in the act of washing his
hands.

Pilate had also made another attempt to save Jesus[as]. He gave
the enraged crowds an option either to save Jesus'[as] life or that of a
notorious criminal called Barabbas (Matt 27:16–17). This provides
us with a significant clue to the state of Pilate's mind at that time.
He was quite obviously against the idea of sentencing Jesus[as]. It
was in this psychological state that he fixed Friday afternoon to be
the day and time of the execution. What actually happened was a
clear indication that he did it on purpose because the Sabbath was
not very far from Friday afternoon and he, as the custodian of law,
knew better than anyone else that before the Sabbath began by
sunset, Jesus'[as] body would have to be taken down; and that is
exactly what happened. What normally took three days and
nights, approximately, to finally inflict a torturous death upon a
condemned man was subjected to Jesus[as] for a few hours at the
most Hardly enough, one is compelled to wonder, to actually kill
a man like Jesus[as], whom an austere life had toughened physically.

Could this incident not be a key to the enigma of Jonah^{as}? As it was a common practice for a condemned person to hang on the cross for three days and nights, this rings a bell indeed in one's mind about the similitude between Jesus^{as} and Jonah^{as}, as mentioned earlier. Jonah^{as} is also supposed to have remained within the body of the fish for three days and three nights. Maybe he too was delivered alive by God's design within three hours instead of three days. So what happened in the case of Jesus^{as} becomes a mirror reflecting and replaying the tragic drama of Jonah^{as}.

Now we turn to the events during the Crucifixion. Even at the last moment Jesus^{as} stood firm to his protestations: *'Eli, Eli, la'ma sabach-tha'ni?'* How deeply tragic this is, and how painfully expressive of his disillusionment. This exclamation is subtly pointing at some earlier promise and assurance which God must have given him; otherwise, no sense whatsoever can be read in this exclamation. It is a denial both of his wish and willingness to carry, of his own volition, the load of other people's sin and of the view that he was looking forward to that hour of death. Why this deep cry of anguish when the punishment was demanded by him in the first place? Why should he reproach God, or even pray for deliverance? Jesus'^{as} statement should be read in the context of what happened before. He was praying to God throughout to take the bitter cup off from him.

We as Aḥmadi Muslims believe that a pious and holy person that Jesus^{as} was, made it impossible that God did not accept his prayer. He must have been told that the prayer had been accepted. I do not believe that he gave up the ghost on the cross. With me there is no contradiction and everything is consistent.

His perceived death was only the impression of an observer who was neither a physician nor had any opportunity to medically examine him. An onlooker, watching with such anxiety and concern lest death should overtake his beloved master, merely observed the dropping of the tired head with chin resting against the chest of Jesus[as]. And 'Lo', he exclaimed, 'He gave up the ghost'. But as we explained earlier, this is not a treatise to discuss the merits and authenticities of the Biblical account from the point of view of genuineness or otherwise, or to dispute any interpretations attributed to them. We are here only to critically examine the very logic and commonsense of Christian philosophy and dogma. The point which is conclusively established therefore is that whether Jesus[as] swooned or died, his painful surprise at what was about to happen strongly proves that he expected otherwise. If death it was that he sought then the surprise that he showed had no justification at all. Our interpretation as Aḥmadi Muslims is that Jesus[as] was only surprised because he was given a promise of deliverance from the cross by God during his supplications the night before. But God had other plans: He caused Jesus[as] to merely swoon so that the sentries on guard could be misled to believe that he had died and as such to release his body to Joseph of Arimathea, to be delivered to his kith and kin. The surprise which we notice in the last words of Jesus Christ[as] was also shared by Pilate himself: 'Already dead', is what he exclaimed when the incident of death was reported to him (Mark 15:44). He must have had a long experience with crucifixion during his tenure as Governor of Judea and could not have expressed his surprise unless he was convinced that it is unusual for death to overtake a crucified person within the short period of only a few hours. Yet he had to accept the plea to release the body under mysterious circumstances. That is why he is forever accused of conspiracy. It is alleged that under the influence of his wife he saw to it that the execution of Jesus[as] took place at an hour very close to the hour of Sabbath. Secondly, he conceded to the request to release the body despite doubtful reports of Jesus'[as] death. This decision of Pilate caused grave concern among the Jews who petitioned him and expressed their doubts and suspicions regarding the death of Jesus[as] (Matt 27:62–66).

We also learn from the Bible that when his body was taken down his legs were not broken, whereas the legs of the two thieves, hanging along with him, were broken to make sure that they died (John 19:31–32). This act of sparing Jesus[as] would certainly have helped his revival from the coma. It cannot be ruled out altogether that the sentries had been instructed by some emissaries of Pilate, not to break the legs of Jesus Christ[as]. Perhaps this was done as a mark of respect for him and the innocent Christian community.

According to the Bible, when his side was pierced blood and water gushed out: But when they came to Jesus[as] and found him already dead, they did not break his legs. Instead one of the soldiers pierced Jesus'[as] side with a spear bringing a sudden flow of blood and water (John 19:33–34).

If he was dead and his heart had stopped beating, such active bleeding as would cause the blood to rush out or gush out would be impossible. At most, coagulated blood and plasma could have passively seeped out. But that is not the picture which the New

Testament presents, it says that blood and water rushed out. As far as the mention of water is concerned it should not be surprising for Jesus[as] to have developed pleurisy during the extremely exacting and punishing hours of trial that he spent upon the cross. Also, the stress of the Crucifixion could have resulted in exudates from the pleura to collect likes bags of water, which is medically termed as wet pleurisy. This condition, which is otherwise dangerous and painful, seems to have turned into an advantage for Jesus[as] because when his side was pierced the swollen pleura could easily have played the role of a cushion protecting the chest organs from being directly penetrated by the spear. Water mixed with blood rushed out because of an active heart.

Another piece of evidence is as follows. According to the Biblical account, after the body was handed over to Joseph of Arimathea, it was immediately removed to a secret place of burial, a sepulchre with enough room not only for Jesus[as] but also for two of his attendants to sit and take care of him: Then the disciples went back to their homes, but Mary[as] stood outside the tomb crying. As she wept, she bent down over to look into the tomb and saw two angels in white, seated where Jesus'[as] body had been (John 20:10–12).

That is not all, we are informed in the New Testament that an ointment, which had been prepared in advance, was applied to Jesus'[as] wounds (John 19:39–40). This ointment, prepared by the disciples of Jesus[as], contained ingredients which have properties of healing wounds and subduing pain etc. Why was there all this fuss about going through the laborious exercise of collecting twelve rare ingredients to prepare an ointment at all? The prescription used is recorded in many classical books such as the famous medical textbook *Al-Qānūn* by Bū 'Ali Sinā (see Appendix I for a list of such books). So what was the need of applying ointment to a dead body? This could only make sense if the disciples had strong reasons to believe that Jesus[as] would be delivered alive from the cross and not dead. St John is the only apostle who has ventured to offer an explanation justifying the act of preparing and applying an ointment to Jesus'[as] body. This further supports the fact that the act of applying ointment to a dead body was considered extremely odd behaviour, inexplicable to those who believed that Jesus[as] was dead when ointment was applied. It is for this reason that St John had to offer an explanation. He suggests that it was done merely because it was a Jewish practice to apply some sort of balm or ointment to the bodies of their dead. Now it is a very important fact to note that all modern scholars who have researched into this are in agreement that St John was not of Jewish origin, and he proved it by this statement of his. It is known for certain that Jews or the Children of Israel have never applied any ointments whatsoever to the bodies of their dead. As such the scholars contend that St John must have been of non-Jewish origin otherwise he could not have been so ignorant of Jewish customs. So there has to be another reason for this.

The ointment was applied to save Jesus[as] from near death. The only explanation lies in the fact that Jesus[as] was neither expected to die by his disciples nor did he actually die upon the cross. The body which was taken down must have shown positive signs of life before the application of the ointment; otherwise, it turns out to be an extremely stupid, unwarranted and futile exercise on the part of those who indulged in it. It is unlikely that those who had prepared this ointment in advance had done so without a very strong indication that Jesus^{as} would not die upon the cross but would be taken down alive seriously wounded very much in need of a powerful healing agent.

It should be borne in mind that the location of the sepulchre where Jesus^{as} lay was kept a closely guarded secret, known to a few of his disciples. This was obviously for the reason that he was still alive and was not yet out of danger.

As for what happened in the sepulchre, this is debatable on many counts; it cannot stand critical examination, and neither can it prove that the person who walked out had really died and had subsequently been resurrected. The only evidence we have is the belief of Christians that the Jesus^{as} who walked out of the sepulchre possessed the same body, which was crucified; bearing the same marks and wounds. If he were seen walking out in the same body, then the only logical conclusion, which could be drawn, would be that he had never died.

Another piece of evidence pointing to the continuity of Jesus'^{as} life is as follows. After three days and three nights he is seen, not by the public, but only by his Disciples, in other words, by people whom he trusted. He avoids the light of day and only meets them under the cover of darkness at night. One may safely infer from the Biblical account that he seems to be moving away from the source of danger with a sense of urgency and secrecy. The question is, if he had been given a new and eternal life after his first death, and was not to suffer another, why was he hiding from the eyes of his enemies; that is, both the government agencies and the

public? He should have appeared to the Jews and the representatives of the Roman Empire and said: 'Here I am, with an eternal
life, try and kill me again if you may, you will never be able to.' But
he preferred to remain hidden. Not that the idea of appearing in
public was not suggested to him, on the contrary, it was specifi-
cally suggested to him to reveal himself to the world, but he
refused and continued to distance himself from Judea so that no
one could follow him.

*Judas (not Iscariot) said to him, "Lord, how is it that you will
manifest yourself to us, and not to the world?" (John 14:22)*

*So they drew near to the village to which they were going. He
appeared to be going further, but they constrained him, saying,
"Stay with us, for it is toward evening and the day is now far
spent." So he went in to stay with them. (Luke 24:28–29)*

This very strongly presents the case of a mortal who is not beyond the reach of death or injury to his person. It only signifies
that Jesus[as] had not died in the sense that he was delivered of the
human element in him but he remained exactly the same in his
nature, whatever it was, and there was no death separating his old
self from the new. This is what we call continuity of life in human
experience. A spirit or a ghost belonging to another world certainly does not behave like Jesus[as] behaved during his secret
meetings under the cover of night with his close friends and
followers.

None other than Jesus[as] himself emphatically rules out the question of Jesus[as] being a ghost When he appeared to some of his

disciples, they could not hide their fear of him because they believed him to be not Jesus[as] himself, but a ghost of Jesus[as]. Jesus Christ[as] understanding their difficulties dispelled their fears by denying being a ghost, asserting he was the same Jesus[as] who was crucified and even invited them to examine his wounds, which were still fresh (John 20:19–27). His appearance to his disciples etc, by no means established his revival from the dead. All that it established was simply his survival from the throes of death.

As if to remove any misunderstanding that might still have lurked in their minds he asked them what they were eating. When he was told that they were eating bread and fish he asked for some of it because he was hungry and ate some (Luke 24:41–42). That certainly is a proof beyond a shadow of doubt against his revival from death, that is, a revival of the nature of a human being having died once and brought to life again. The problems arising out of such an understanding of the revival of Jesus Christ[as] would be two-fold.

If Jesus[as] was still the god–human species, as he is claimed to have been before his crucifixion, then he could not have got rid of the man inside him. This presents a very complicated and problematic situation. What did death do to him, or them, that is the man in Jesus[as] and the god in him? Did the souls of both man and god depart together and return to the same earthly body again, having visited the same hell together, or was it only the soul of the god in Jesus[as] which returned to the human body without the soul of man? Where did that soul disappear to, one is left wondering. Was his journey to hell a journey of no return, while the godly soul in him was confined therein only for three days and nights? Was God the Father of the man Jesus[as] or the Son Jesus[as]? This question has to be settled once and for all to give us a clear picture. Was the body of Jesus[as], partially a body of God and partially a body of man?

The concept of God which we have been granted by the study of both the Old Testament and the New Testament is that of an incorporeal infinite being, with matter having played no role in the making of His person. Having understood this much, let us look back at Jesus[as] as he was going through different stages of development as an embryo in the womb of Mary[as]. All the matter which went into the making of Jesus[as] has to be contributed by the human mother with not even an iota of it being supplied by God the Father. Of course God could have created him miraculously. But from my point of view, creation, whether it appears to be, miraculous or natural, is still creation. We can only accept someone to be the father of a son if the substance of the father and the substance of the mother are both shared equally or partially so that at least some of the substance of the body of the child is derived from the substance of the father.

From this it should become very clear to the reader that God did not play any fatherly role at all in the birth process of the human embryo and the entire corporeal body with all its cardiac, respiratory, alimentary, portal, cellular and central nervous systems was the unaided product of the human mother alone. Where is the element of sonship in Jesus[as] who was merely a receptacle for the soul of God and no more? This new understanding of the relationship between God and Jesus[as] can be sensibly described as anything but a father-son relationship.

CHAPTER FIVE

REVIVAL OR RESURRECTION?

THE SCENARIO OF JESUS'[as] REVIVAL FROM THE DEAD presents many problems. Some of them have already been discussed in the previous chapter. Now we turn to other elements and complexities. What we have in view is the nature of the 'mind' of Jesus[as], prior to the Crucifixion and after his revival from the dead. His mind was brought to life again, after a loss of function for three days and nights. The question is, what actually happens to the brain at the time of death? On one point at least there is a consensus among both the Christian and the non-Christian medical experts: if the brain remains dead for more than a few minutes, it is dead and gone forever. As soon as the blood supply ceases, the brain begins to disintegrate.

If Jesus[as] died during the Crucifixion it can only mean that his heart ceased functioning and stopped supplying blood to his brain, and that his brain died soon after. So his entire life support system must have stopped operating, or he could not have been declared dead. That being so we are faced with a very intriguing problem in relation to the understanding of the life and death of Jesus Christ[as].

The death of Jesus Christ[as], as has been demonstrated, would mean a final departure of his astral body, or soul as we may call it, from the physical cage of his human body. If so, his revival would have to mean the return of the same astral body to the same physical body that it had left behind three days earlier. Such a return of the soul would restart the clock of physical life and set it ticking once again. For such a thing to happen, the disintegrated and dead brain cells would have to come to life suddenly and the chemical processes of rapid decay would have to be reversed entirely. This involves an enormous problem and will ever remain a challenge for the Christian biochemists to resolve. Describing the reversal of the entire chemical processes of decay within the central nervous system is beyond the reach of the farthest stretches of scientist's imagination. If it ever happened it would be a miracle indeed, defying science and making a mockery of the laws made by God Himself, but it would be a miracle that would still fail to solve the problem at hand.

Such a revival would mean not just the revival of the cells of the central nervous system, but actually their synthesis. Even if the same cells were reconstructed and brought to life exactly as they were before, they would, in fact, be a new set of cells devoid of any previous memory. They would have to be re-manufactured, complete with all the data relevant to the life of Jesus[as] that was wiped out of his brain after the death of his mind.

Life, as we know it, comprises a consciousness that is filled with information held by billions of neurons within the brain. That information is then subdivided into far more complicated and interrelated bits of computerised information received from each of the five senses. If that data were wiped out, life itself would be wiped out. Therefore, the revival of the brain of Jesus[as] would mean the construction and the manufacture of a new brain computer with a completely new set of software. This complexity also relates to the chemistry of the rest of the body of Jesus Christ[as]. To revive the body, a colossal chemical reconstruction process would have to be put into operation after retrieving all the material lost in the process of decay. With such a great miracle having taken place the question would arise as to who was revived and with what effect? Was it the man in Jesus[as], or was it the god in him? This is why we are emphasising the importance of understanding the person of Jesus[as].

Whenever Jesus[as] is known to have faltered and failed to exhibit his superpowers as the Son of God, Christians take refuge in the claim that he faltered as a man and not as a god. So we have every right to question and to clearly define which part in him was man and which was god. The faltering of the man in Jesus[as] requires a human mind as a separate entity to that of the god in him. When the brain was revived it was the human element in Jesus[as] which was revived because the 'Divine' entity of Jesus[as] did not require a material brain to support him. For the 'Divine' entity it only worked as a receptacle during his previous sojourn on earth, as in the case of a spiritual medium. Hence, the revival of Jesus[as] would only imply the revival of the man in him, without which the return of his spirit to the same body is rendered impossible.

If this scenario is not acceptable then we will face another grave problem of attributing to Jesus[as] during his earthly life two independent minds, one of man and another that of god, with the two minds cohabiting the same space but otherwise unrelated and independent. If so, the revival issue will have to be re-examined so that its true nature is clearly understood. In this scenario, one does not have to conceive of the essential reconstruction of the human brain to provide a seat for the human mind; we need only to imagine Jesus^{as} revisiting a skull filled with the decaying remains of the brain of his former human host

The deeper we look into this problem, more problems raise their heads at every newly probed level. Man's mind requires a brain as a tool of his thought process. As far as the functions of the physical body are concerned, if we believe that the mind is a separate entity which lives by itself, then this would imply that the mind and the soul are the same thing. By whatever name we refer to it, whether we call it mind or soul, it may be considered as capable of living separately even when its relationship with the human brain is severed. But if the mind or the soul is required to govern the human body, or to be influenced by what goes on in its physical realms then there has to be a profound bondage between the mind and the brain, or the soul and the brain, otherwise they simply cannot influence, motivate or control the physical, mental or sentimental processes in man. Perhaps this is not debatable.

From this we are led to another serious problem: does the so-called Divine Son need to control a body through a brain? And does he depend on a physical brain for his thought processes? If he transcends all human limitations and if he has an independent system of thought processes, unique to him, with no parallel in the entire universe of his creation, then the return of the soul of God to the human body along with that of the mind of man reconstructs a bizarre situation of a dual personality with two conflicting thought processes, because it is impossible for the human mind and the human soul to be completely at one with the mind of God and His being. There would be a constant variation between the two thought processes with very irritating clashes of brain waves. Such a case would be fit to be treated by a superhuman psychiatrist It is a new type of spiritual schizophrenia, perhaps.

Having said that, let us reconstruct the entire scenario from a different angle. After studying Christianity at some depth I have come to the conclusion that there is confusion prevailing in the understanding of some terms and their application, without fully understanding their implications, to situations where they do not actually apply. Christian ideology is densely befogged with such confusion and misapplied terminology. 'Revival' is one term and 'Resurrection' is another, and both have different meanings. So far, we have intentionally used the term 'revival' when discussing the possibility of Jesus[as] coming to life again. As we have clearly seen from the previous discussion 'revival' means the return of all vital functions of the human body after death. But 'resurrection' is a completely different phenomenon.

Unfortunately, the Christian church, all over the world, has been responsible for creating confusion in Christian minds by misusing these terms by swapping one with the other, or at least by attributing the meaning of one to the other. Most Christians understand the resurrection of Jesus Christ[as] as the springing to life once again of his human body which he had abandoned at the moment of his so-called death. Of course we disagree with this and retain our right to describe it as a state of deep coma and not death.

If correctly understood and applied, the phrase 'resurrection of Jesus[as]' cannot mean the return of his soul to the same human body which it had deserted at the moment of death. The term 'resurrection' only means the creation of a new astral body. Such a body is spiritual in nature and works as a sort of crucible for a rarefied soul within. It is created for the eternal continuation of life after death. Some call it a sidereal body or astral body and some call it *Atma* [Atman]. Whatever name you give it the essential meaning remains the same; resurrection applies to the creation of a new body for the soul which is ethereal in nature and not, we repeat, not, the return of the soul to the same disintegrated human body which it left previously.

St Paul has spoken at length in exactly these terms about the resurrection of Jesus Christ[as]. He believed in the resurrection of not only Jesus[as] but the resurrection in general of all those who die and are deemed fit by God to be given a new existence and a new form of life. The personality of the soul remains the same but its abode is changed. According to St Paul, this is a general phenomenon which has to be accepted, otherwise there would be no meaning left in Christianity or religion.

St Paul's letters to the Corinthians must be studied in depth because they are central to the issue. They leave no room for doubt, in my mind at least, that whenever he spoke of Jesus[as] having been seen alive after the Crucifixion he spoke clearly and without ambiguity of his resurrection and resurrection alone, and it never crossed his mind that the soul of Jesus[as] had returned to his mortal body and that he was resuscitated from death in ordinary physical terms. If my understanding of St Paul is not acceptable to some Christian theologians, they will have to admit that St Paul glaringly contradicted himself because at least in some of his accounts of Jesus'[as] new life he leaves no shadow of doubt that he understood Jesus'[as] new life to be the resurrection and not revival of the human body in which his soul is said to have been caged.

Following are some of the relevant passages which speak for themselves:

And God raised the Lord and will also raise us up by his power. (1 Corinthians 6:14)

So is it with the resurrection of the dead. What is sown is perishable, what is raised is imperishable. It is sown in dishonor, it is raised in glory. It is sown in weakness, it is raised in power. It is sown a physical body, it is raised a spiritual body. If there is a physical body, there is also a spiritual body. (Ibid 15:42–44)

Lo! I tell you a mystery. We shall not all sleep, but we shall all be changed, in a moment, in the twinkling of an eye, at the last trumpet. For the trumpet will sound, and the dead will be raised imperishable, and we shall be changed. (Ibid 15:51–52)

We are of good courage, and we would rather be away from the body and at home with the Lord. (2 Corinthians 5:8)

The problem which remains to be resolved arises out of St Paul's reference to the early Christian account of how Jesus[as] was seen alive in his body soon after the Crucifixion. If St Paul understood Jesus^{as} to have been resurrected, he could be right, of course, and his personal 'vision' of Jesus^{as} or communion with him could be explained in terms of resurrection like the visiting soul of a dead person from the other world, acquiring an apparition very much like its form and shape prior to death. But there seems to be confusion over the mixing up of two types of evidence. Firstly we need to consider the early evidence of his disciples and of those who loved and revered him, although they might not have been formally initiated into Christianity. That evidence must have been misunderstood by St Paul because it clearly speaks of Jesus^{as} in his human form with a corporeal body that cannot be interpreted as resurrection.

To prove this, one has only to refer to the episode of Jesus^{as} surprising some of his disciples:

> *But they were startled and frightened, and supposed that they saw a spirit. And he said to them, "Why are you troubled, and why do questionings rise in your hearts? See my hands and my feet, that it is I myself; handle me, and see; for a spirit has not flesh and bones as you see that I have." And while they still disbelieved for joy, and wondered he said to them, "Have you anything here to eat?" They gave him a piece of broiled fish, and he took it and ate before them. (Luke 24:37–43)*

This episode categorically rules out the idea of resurrection, and speaks of Jesus^{as} wanting to demonstrate clearly that he was the same person in the same human body and not a ghost; nor was he someone no longer dependant on food for survival. This further shows that the early Christians were speaking of two different things. Whenever they spoke of the revival of Jesus[as] from the dead and were confronted by the sceptical regarding the sheer absurdity of the idea, they took refuge in the notion of resurrection, which could be philosophically and logically explained. Corinthians, in particular, presents an excellent opportunity to study the dilemma of putting one's feet in two different boats.

Finally returning to the evidence of the early Christian's encounters with Jesus Christ[as], we are left with no option but to believe that the Jesus[as] who appeared soon after the Crucifixion to many of his disciples and friends, who spoke to them, who accompanied them and moved gradually away from the scene of the Crucifixion, mostly under the cover of night was certainly not a resurrected person but one who could only be taken as a person who was either physically revived from the dead, or one who never died but was miraculously recovered from a state of near death. He was so near, indeed, to death that his state could be compared to the state of Jonah[as] in the belly of the fish. We have no doubt in our minds that this latter option is the only acceptable one.

To make it easier for Christians to understand our point of view I will present a similar hypothetical case. The same story is repeated in real life today. An attempt is made to kill someone by crucifying him and he is supposed to be dead as a result. Afterwards, the same person is seen moving about by some of his close associates. They also observe that his physical body visibly carries the marks of crucifixion. He is then recaptured by the Law and presented to a court of justice with a demand from the prosecution that as he had somehow escaped death in the first attempt so as to consummate the sentence passed against him, he must be crucified once again. That man then defends himself by postulating that he most certainly has died once; hence the purpose of law is indeed achieved and now that he had risen from the dead by a special decree of God so the past judgement of condemnation could not be re-executed for the reason that he is enjoying a completely new lease of life in which he had committed no offence against the law. If the court accepts this plea, obviously he would not be punished again for a crime for which he had already paid his dues.

If such an incident were to happen in a court of law in a Christian country with a Christian judge and a Christian jury, what verdict would the reader suggest they would or should pass? If the plea of the person under trial is to be rejected and he is condemned to be hanged again, on what grounds would it be justified?

Evidently, any sane judge, Christian or non-Christian, and any jury made up of sane people would not even remotely entertain the plea that having died once the accused had come to life again. Such a verdict has no parochial, religious, racial or ethnic bias. It is universal in nature and no man in command of his sanity can think of a verdict other than this. Hence the universal consensus of human intellect would reject the plea of 'revival', and would only pass a verdict of 'survival' from death. That is exactly what happened in the case of Jesus Christ[as]. It was neither a case of revival, nor of resurrection, but simply as common sense would have it, a clear case of survival.

The coming to life of the dead body of Jesus[as] is so essential to Christianity that one has to investigate the real reasons behind it. Apparently there is no logic in the entire episode. Why should a so-called 'Son of God', having been once delivered from his human cage, ever choose to return to it? And how could it be taken as proof beyond doubt that he had actually died and had then come to life again? This aspect has already been considered at some length and I am not attempting to emphasize the same point, but I wish to draw the reader's attention to another vital relevant question.

Why did such an absurd idea take root in Christian theology, and gradually in a few centuries after Jesus[as], grow into one of the pillars of Christian belief, without which the whole edifice of Christian theology would collapse? We will try to project ourselves into the minds of the early Christians who faced an almost insoluble dilemma, and began to reconstruct the circumstances in which Christianity was given a shape different from its reality. This way perhaps it will be easier for us to understand, in depth, the making and unmaking of Christianity. The hard fact which must be brought into sharp focus is simply this: if Jesus[as], peace be upon him, did actually die upon the cross then in the eyes of the Jewish people he would clearly appear to be an impostor.

Vitriolic Language against Holy People

As referred to earlier, the scriptures had predicted that any false claimant, who attributed anything to God which He had not said, would hang upon the tree. Therefore the death of Jesus[as] upon the cross would be tantamount to the death of Christianity. That is why authentic Jewish religious literature is full of gloatings about Jesus'[as] death upon the cross. He was considered to have been proved false, beyond a shadow of doubt, by his contemporary Jewish adversaries on the basis of that particular Biblical verdict. They lost even a semblance of respect for him and used such filthy and insulting language against him that it is an unbearable reading for anyone who loves Jesus[as] as we do, as a true, beloved and holy messenger of Allah. One can well imagine the deep suffering and intense agony of the early Christians who had known Jesus[as] to be a holy man and a true messenger of God, having been assigned the special station of the Messiah[as]. How would they defend themselves against the onslaught of such filthy language which, when read today in the present day context, brings to mind the ugly image of Salman Rushdie's notorious book *The Satanic Verses?*

Such total lack of respect for decency by both seems to have arisen from the depths of human degradation. The following quotes will give the reader some idea as to what happens to all decent human values when the rabid antagonists of holy people choose to make them a target of their impudent, perverted and distorted ravings.

The Talmud, the doctrinal book which fully expounds all the knowledge and beliefs of the Jewish people, taught that Jesus[as] had not only an illegitimate birth, but was doubly uncouth in view of his having been born out of a devilish wedlock of Mary[as] during the period of her menstruation. It further elaborated that he had the soul of Esau; that he was a fool, a conjurer, a seducer; that he was crucified, buried in hell and set up as an idol ever since by his followers. The extracts which follow have been taken from the book *The Talmud Unmasked*, by Reverend I.B. Pranaitis.

"The following is narrated in the Tract Kallah, lb *(18b):*

'Once when the Elders were seated at the Gate, two young men passed by, one of whom had his head covered. The other with his head bare. Rabbi Eliezer remarked that the one in his bare head was illegitimate, a mamzer. *Rabbi Jehoschua said that he was conceived during menstruation,* ben niddah. *Rabbi Akibah, however, said that he was both. Whereupon the others asked Rabbi Akibah why he dared to contradict his colleagues. He answered that he could prove what he said. He went therefore to the boy's mother whom he saw sitting in the market place selling vegetables and said to her: 'My daughter, if you will answer truthfully what I am going to ask you, I promise that you will be saved in the next life.' She demanded that he would swear to keep his promise, and Rabbi Akibah did so—but with his lips only, for in his heart he invalidated his oath. Then he said: 'Tell me what kind of son is this of yours?' To which she replied: 'The day I was married I was having menstruation, and because of this my husband left me. But an evil spirit came and slept with me and from this intercourse my son was born to me.' Thus it was proved that this young man was not only illegitimate but also conceived during the menstruation of his mother. And when his questioners heard this they declared: 'Great indeed was Rabbi Akibah when he corrected his Elders!'*

And they exclaimed: 'Blessed be the Lord God of Israel, who revealed his secret to Rabbi Akibah the son of Joseph!'"

That the Jews understand this story to refer to Jesus and his mother, Mary, is clearly demonstrated in their book Toldath Jeschu— *'The Generation of Jesus'—where the birth of our Saviour is narrated in almost the same words*.'"*

All that is decent in man revolts against the stinking filth which was heaped upon the holy name and image of Jesus[as] in the literature of his hostile antagonists. Of course, Jesus[as] was conceived by a chaste holy lady named Mary[as], and nothing else played a role in that conception but the limitless creative powers of our Lord God. The idea of conception by intercourse with the devil during the state of menstruation is far more aptly applicable to the mind that conceived this enormity. Alas, neither the holy spouses of holy people nor even their mothers are spared by the tongues and pens of perverts who spit venom and ugliness alike. It does not make any difference whether such a maniac lived two thousand years ago, or was born in the contemporary world. How amazing it is that even the most civilized societies of today can shut their eyes to this beastliness, and would rather approve of such flagrant offences in the name of liberty of tongue and pen.

---

* The Talmud Unmasked' by Rev I.B. Pranaitis, Chap. I, p.30.

The language used by Salman Rushdie, for instance, against the holy ladies of the Holy Prophet[sa] of Islam is not dissimilar to the language used against the holy mother of Christ[as]:

> *"It is also narrated in* Sanhedrin, *67a: 'This is what they did to the son of Stada in Lud, and they hanged him on the eve of the Passover. For this son of Stada was the son of Pandira. For Rabbi Chasda tells us that Pandira was the husband of Stada, his mother, and he lived during the time of Paphus the son of Jehuda.'"*[3]

The author of *The Talmud Unmasked*, Rev I.B. Pranaitis makes the following comment on the verses quoted above:

> *The meaning of this is that this Mary was called Stada, that is, a prostitute, because, according to what was taught at Pumbadita she left her husband and committed adultery. This is also recorded in the Jerusalem Talmud and Maimonides. Whether those who believe such devilish lies deserve greater hatred or pity, I cannot say.*

This indeed is a cry of anguish from the heart of a helpless victim who is grieved by the fanatical mockery of his beloved master. The early Christians must have suffered even greater agony and experienced hell by the mockery of the Jews of that period. They had to suffer invectives, directed not against someone whose memory was long buried in the past, but against someone whose

---

[3] Ibid.

beloved memory was still fresh and alive, and who was profoundly loved by those who had seen him and had shared some most beautiful moments of their lives with him. They would have been doubly tormented, because it was not only the heinous mockery which hurt them but further insult was added to injury by the suffering of Jesus Christ[as] during his conviction and attempted crucifixion. I only wish that the Christian conscience of the free West could at least make some effort to understand the agony and anguish of a billion Muslims who are most certainly not tortured less when similar inhuman language is used against their beloved Holy Master[sa] and his Companions[ra].

The early Christians had to suffer all this despite their personal knowledge and despite possessing irrevocable evidence to the effect that Jesus[as] was alive and that he had not died upon the cross as boasted by the Jews. They had themselves treated his wounds. They had seen him recover miraculously from a deep state of coma in which his body was delivered to them, and had seen him with their own eyes, not in the form of an apparition or a ghost, but in the same frail human body which had suffered so much for the sake of truth and had yet miraculously survived death. They talked with him, ate with him and had seen him moving step by step, night after night in utter secrecy away from the scene of the Crucifixion.

Ascension

The subject of the Ascension of Jesus Christ[as] is untouched by St Matthew and St John in their Gospels. The lack of mention of such an important event leaves one wondering as to why. The only two synoptic Gospels which mention the Ascension are Mark (Mark16:19) and Luke (Luke 24:51). However, recent scientific and scholarly investigations have proved that the accounts contained in both these Gospels are later interpolations. These verses were non-existent in the original texts.

Codex Sinaiticus dates from the 4th century and remains the oldest near complete text of the Old and New Testament[*]. It stands witness to the fact that the said verses in both Mark and Luke were not included in the authentic original versions, but were certainly added by some scribe on his own initiative much later. In the Codex Sinaiticus the Gospel of Mark ends at chapter 16 verse 8. This fact is now acknowledged in some modern Bible editions as well[*]. Also, the Gospel of Luke (24: 15) in Codex Sinaiticus, does not contain the words 'taken up into heaven.'

According to the textual critic C.S.C. Williams, if these omissions in the Codex Sinaiticus are correct, there is no reference at all to the Ascension in the original text of the Gospels.[*]

Even Jehovah's Witnesses, who are some of the most vehement proponents of Jesus[as] 'Sonship' and his ascent to God the Father,

---

[*] Jesus the Evidence by Ian Wilson (1984), p 18.
[*] The Holy Bible, New International Version (1984) by International Bible Society, p 1024.
[*] The Secrets of Mount Sinai, the Story of Finding the World's Oldest Bible Codex Sinaiticus, by James Bently, p. 131.

had to admit ultimately that the verses in Mark and Luke are additions without a foundation in the original texts.[*]

What Happened to Jesus' Body?

A closer critical examination from the point of view of common sense and logic reveals further absurdities inherent in the episodes of the Crucifixion and the Ascension as presented by the Christians of today. As far as the question of Jesus'[as] return to his human body is concerned, enough has been said. We only want to add to the issue of what might have happened to that body when Jesus[as] finally ascended, if he ever did.

When confronted by the question as to what happened to the body of Jesus Christ[as], it is suggested by some Christians that as he ascended to his heavenly Father his carnal body disintegrated and disappeared in a glow. This raises a fundamental question. If the departure of Jesus[as] from the human body was to result in such an explosive event, why did it not happen at the instant of his first reported death? The only reference we have in the Bible to Jesus'[as] death is when he was still hanging on the cross and in the words of St Matthew 'he gave up the ghost' Apparently, nothing happened other than a smooth departure of the soul from the body. Are we to assume that he did not die upon the cross after all, because if he had left the body, it should have exploded in a

---

[*] New World Translation.

similar fashion even then? Why did it only happen the second time Jesus[as] left his body? Under the circumstances only two avenues are open to proceed further:

1. That the person of Jesus[as] did not remain eternally confined to the human body after his soul returned to it and that during his ascent he cast away his human body and ascended purely as a spirit of God.

This is neither supported by facts nor is it conceivable because that would lead into a blind alley of believing that Jesus[as] died twice. The first time on the cross and the second time on Ascension.

2. That he remained confined within the human shell eternally.

This cannot be accepted because it is utterly repulsive and inconsistent with the dignity and majesty of the image of God. On the other hand, we have a point of view of common sense; 'It would be a mistake to understand Jesus'[as] ascension as a sort of ancient space trip, and heaven as a place beyond the sun, moon and the galaxies. The truth is neither here nor there.[4] The concoction of such a bizarre story, therefore, could only have been motivated by the insoluble dilemma that the Christians faced during the nascent period of Christianity. When Jesus[as] disappeared from view, naturally the question would have been raised as to what happened to him. The early Christians could not have

---

[4] The Lion Handbook of Christian Belief, Lion, London (1982) p. 120.

resolved the quandary by openly professing that as he had never died so there was no question of a body being left behind and that his body had in fact gone along with him during the course of his migration. In this way the problem of the disappearance of the body could have been easily resolved. But this confession was impossible to make. Those who would have dared to admit that Jesus[as] was seen alive and gradually moving away from Judea faced the peril of being condemned by the Roman Law as accessories to the crime of escape from justice.

To seek refuge in the concoction of a story, like the ascent of Jesus[as] to heaven offered a safer option, however bizarre the idea. Yet of course it would involve indulgence in falsehood. We must pay our tribute to the integrity of the early disciples who despite this predicament did not seek refuge in a false statement. All writers of the Gospels chose to remain silent on this issue rather than take refuge behind a smoke screen of misstatements. No doubt they must have suffered the jeering of their adversaries, but they chose to suffer in silence.

Mysterious silence on the part of those who knew the inside story must have been largely responsible for sowing the seeds of doubt in the minds of Christians of later generations. They must have wondered: why, after the soul of Jesus Christ[as] had departed, was there no mention of his body being left behind? Where had it gone and what had happened to it? Why did the soul of Christ[as] return to the same body if it ever did? These vital but unanswered questions could have given birth to other questions. If revival meant returning to the same body, what must have happened to Jesus Christ[as] after the second term of his imprisonment in the carnal human frame? Did he eternally remain locked up in that body, never to be released again?

On the other hand if the soul of Jesus[as] once again departed from the same body, then was that revival temporary or permanent? If he did not remain locked in it then what happened to his body after his second death? Where was it buried and is there any mention of it in any archives or chronicles?

It seems that these questions, even if not raised earlier, must have been raised during the later centuries when intense philosophical exercises concerning the mystery of Christ[as] and all about him were witnessed widely among Christian theologians. It appears that some unscrupulous scribe tried to wriggle out of this by interpolating the last twelve verses in the Gospel of St Mark, and falsely attributed to him the statement that Jesus[as] was last seen ascending to heaven in the same body.

The hands of concoction did not spare the Gospel of Luke either, where the clever insertion of the words 'and he was carried up to heaven' in 24:51 served the purpose of the interpolator. In this way he put to rest the queries once and for all. At least one mystery of Christian dogma was thus resolved. But alas, at what cost! At the cost of the noble facts relating to the real holy image of Jesus Christ[as]. The fact of Christ[as] was thus sacrificed on the altar of fiction. From then on, Christianity continued to proceed unabated and unchecked in the journey of his transformation from facts to fiction. We know for certain that the Jews were unhappy and disturbed at not finding the body of Jesus Christ[as] (Matt 28:11–15). They wanted to be sure of Jesus'[as] death and for that they needed the universally acceptable proof of death, that is, the presence of a dead body. Their complaint, lodged with Pilate, evidently displays their uneasiness about its potential disappearance (Matt 27:62–64).

The real and simple answer, however, lay in the fact that as Christ[as] had not died in the manner that was believed, so the question of a missing body was totally irrelevant, and in keeping with his promise he must have left Judea in search of the lost sheep of the House of Israel. Obviously he could not be seen again.

The Aḥmadiyya Muslim Viewpoint

The Aḥmadiyya Muslim viewpoint of the whereabouts of Jesus'[as] body is very clear, logical and factual. It presents Jesus[as] and what happened to him in the light of truth, haloed by its glory. The very reality of Jesus Christ[as] is so beautiful that there is no need to build an ornamental mystery around him. His reality encompasses his suffering for the sake of sinful humanity throughout his life, which culminated in the agony of the Crucifixion; his deliverance from the cross as promised by the Merciful and Beneficent God Almighty, and his subsequent migration in pursuit of the ten lost tribes of Israel.

Hence he delivered the message of God not only to the two tribes whom he addressed before the Crucifixion, but he also reached out to all the other tribes of Israel and thus fulfilled the purpose of his commission. It was only then that he brought the full purpose of his ministry to a final end. These are the noble and illustrious realities of Jesus'[as] life.

The founder of the Aḥmadiyya Community, Ḥaḍrat Mirza Ghulam Aḥmad[as] of Qadian declared about a hundred years ago that Jesus[as], a true prophet of God, was delivered from the cross as was implied in his earlier discourses. For the first time in the history of Islam, Ḥaḍrat Mirza Ghulam Aḥmad, divinely guided as he was, lifted the mystical veil from the brilliant realities of Jesus'[as] life. It was he who declared in the face of the bitter resentment of the majority of the orthodox Muslims that Jesus[as] had neither died upon the cross, nor ascended bodily to heaven, but was miraculously delivered alive from the cross in keeping with God's promise. Thereafter Jesus[as] migrated in search of the lost sheep of the House of Israel as he himself had promised.

By following the probable route of the migration of Israeli tribes one can safely assume that he must have travelled through Afghanistan on his way to Kashmir and other parts of India where the presence of Israeli tribes was reported.

There is strong historical evidence that the peoples of both Afghanistan and Kashmir have stemmed from migrant Jewish tribes. Ḥaḍrat Mirza Ghulam Aḥmad revealed that Jesus[as] ultimately died and was buried in Srinagar, Kashmir.

When Aḥmadis put forward this explanation as a plausible and realistic solution to the disappearance of Jesus'[as] body from the country of his birth, many a time they are met with the rebuttal that even given that he was delivered from the cross alive, it is extremely far-fetched that he should have taken the hazardous journey from Judea to Kashmir. Hearing this rebuttal Aḥmadis are left wondering as to which distance is longer, the one from Palestine to Kashmir or the one from the Earth to the farthest reaches of Heaven. Again Aḥmadis wonder as to what happened to the promise of Jesus Christ[as] that he would go in search of the Lost Sheep of the House of Israel. If he departed straight from Palestine to sit on the right hand of his Father, did he forget about his commitment, or was his promise impossible for him to keep? It is either this or, as we suggested earlier, should it be expected that the Lost Sheep of the House of Israel had earlier ascended to the heavens where Jesus[as] went in their pursuit?

Survival Cases

For those who still find it difficult to believe that the scenario of Jesus[as] having been delivered alive from the cross is too far-fetched and unacceptable, we draw their attention to the fact that in the light of known and recorded history of man's survival in extremely hazardous situations, the case of Jesus[as], as we have presented it, is neither bizarre nor impossible to accept. Many medically reported and verified cases of near death present a host of evidence in favour of the survival of people in almost impossible situations.

The well documented case of a Maharajah of a small state of pre-partition India is worthy of mention. He was subjected to a similar near impossible situation in which he had few chances of survival. The Maharajah in question was poisoned by his wife and while his body was being cremated with the fires well lit, a violent storm suddenly appeared. Ultimately he not only escaped death but also after a long legal battle was reinstated to his throne. The story runs like this:

"Ramendra Narayan Roy, the Kumar of the Bhowal Estate with headquarters of the Court of Wards at Joydevpur, was alleged to have been poisoned and subsequently declared dead and placed for cremation at the burning ghat in May, 1909. Circumstances suggested that his wife was a principal player in the attempted murder. A heavy thunder burst, before the completion of the cremation, caused the party responsible for burning the dead body to hurriedly return, leaving the dead-body. The rain caused the fire to extinguish. A group of sadhus (Hindu hermits) who were passing by noticed that the man was alive. He was thus rescued. Next day when it was discovered by the conspirators that the body had disappeared, they had another body cremated to make Kumar's death look like a fact.

The sadhus, who had saved him, then took him from place to place. The near death experience had caused Kumar to lose his memory but he regained it gradually and visited Joydevpur twelve years later. The familiar surroundings of his home town caused him to regain his memory entirely. When Kumar filed a civil suit to recover the estate from the Court of Wards as the genuine heir and owner of Bhowal Estate, his wife and some others contested it. A court case was then bitterly fought between the two parties. More than one thousand people gave evidence in favour of Kumar and four hundred in support of his wife. The actual matter being contested was regarding the identity of Kumar as according to common knowledge he had died twelve years ago.

The case was won by Kumar after he identified some marks on the body of his wife which only a husband could have known. His estate was then restored to him."[*]

Hundreds of thousands of similar cases might have gone completely unreported. Thanks to modern medical facilities and media coverage, hundreds of similar cases are being reported and recorded. If all this is plausible in cases of ordinary people from all classes of society and from all sorts of religious moral backgrounds, why could it not be possible in the case of Jesus[as]? If anyone has the chance of surviving in challenging and almost impossible situations, Jesus[as] indeed stands a greater chance because of the special circumstance surrounding him. Strangely enough, however, the sceptics dismiss the suggestion that Jesus[as] did survive the attempted murder by crucifixion. Yet they would readily believe a far more unrealistic, bizarre and unnatural tale of his revival from absolute death—death, which lasted a full three days and nights according to them.

The field of medical research has also taken interest in the phenomenon of near death. A study was carried out in which seventy eight reports of near death experiences were examined. In eighty percent of the cases medical personnel were present during or immediately after these experiences. Interestingly, forty one

---

[*] The Bhowal Case, compiled by J.M. Mitra and R.C. Chakravarty, published by Peer & Son, Calcutta.

percent of the subjects reported that they had been considered dead during the near death experience.[*]

With all kinds of gadgetry at their disposal, if medical experts can pronounce a living person dead, how reliable would be the testimony of an anxious observer who saw Jesus[as] losing consciousness and from this deduced that he had died? Furthermore, after seeing him again, to draw the conclusion that he was revived from death is totally unjustified.

---

[*] The Phenomenology of Near-Death Experiences, by Bruce Greyson, M.D and Ian Stevenson, M.D., AM. Psychiatry 137:10, October 1980

CHAPTER SIX

TRINITY

So far we have only examined the underlying compulsions, which led to the creation of the myths of the deification of Jesus[as] and his so-called role in the Trinity as the Son of God. But the third person in the Christian dogma of Trinity, that is the Holy Ghost, is a bit of an enigma. Why could not 'Two in One' suffice and why was there the need to introduce the third entity into this fundamental doctrine? Logically, the third entity has no justification to occupy a place in the Christian concept of godhead. Harnack, a commentator on this question, feels that, initially, Christianity was represented by a dyad in God and Jesus[as]. It later encompassed the church, referring to it as 'The Spirit,' to add an element of divinity to what would otherwise be a hollow and implausible third partner. This also served an excellent anti-Judaic tool.[*] Rev K.E. Kirk in his essay on 'The Evolution of the Doctrine of Trinity' has this to say on the same subject:

'We naturally turn to the writers of that period to discover what grounds they have for their belief. To our surprise, we are forced to

---

[*] Harnack, 'Constitution and Law of the Church,' E.T. p. 264

admit that they have none. The question as it presented itself to
them was not, Why three persons? But rather Why not?'

He goes on to point out the complete failure of Christian theology to produce any logical justification for the Trinitarian
doctrine and the Christian triad could be explained as essentially a
binary concept to which a third disparate entity was laced in order
to paint a more complete picture.[*]

We believe that this entity gradually evolved under the influence of earlier pagan philosophies and myths which abounded in
the Roman Empire. The exchange of ideas must have drawn
Christian theologians to determine the position of the Holy
Ghost. As there is ample evidence of the existence of such faiths
or cults that visualized God as being composed of three entities in
one, it is not difficult to trace back the ultimate source of the
Christian doctrine of the Trinity. After all if two could be one,
and one could be two, why could not three be one as well? It is
for the research scholars to determine exactly when and how the
third entity of the Christian godhead took its firm roots in Christian mythology, but at present it is outside the domain of this
discussion. Here, we only wish to examine the absurdity of such
claims, which are rejected outright by human understanding.
Human nature spurns self-contradictory and paradoxical ideas.

---

[*] Essays on the Trinity and the Incarnation, p. 93, edited by A. E. J. Rawlinson, Longman,
London 1929.

Interrelationship within Trinity

When one tries to visualize the inter-relationship of the three constituents of the Christian godhead, the only possible scenarios which arise are as follows:

1. They possessed different phases or aspects of one single person.
2. They were three different persons, sharing eternity among them equally.
3. They were three persons with some of their characteristics individual, distinct, and not entirely shared by others.
4. They were three persons in one with completely similar characteristics and similar equal powers, merged with each other and with no functions separate from the other.

We will consider each of these possibilities in turn.

Different Phases or Aspects of One Single Person

As for the first possibility there is no need to discuss it at length because there is hardly any Christian today who would believe Jesus[as] to be an aspect or a phase of God rather than a distinct person. Believers in Trinity insist on there being three different persons merged into one.

The moment one accepts the scenario of one person having different aspects displayed simultaneously, the concept of Trinity, that is, of three gods in one, melts away into thin air, and no Trinity is left at all. Then it would be God the Father Himself who, motivated by His mercy, would die for human sins. In this case it will merely be a transient phase of the same person. Aspects

are not persons, and similarly phases do not create separate entities. Any human being can pass through a multitude of varying
moods and aspects, without splitting into two or three or many
persons. Therefore, if God decided to die for the sake of the sinful
humanity, it would have to be God Himself and not His aspects
who would do so.

Hence, regarding the case in point, that aspect of God which
played a vital role in the Divine sacrifice for the sake of sinful
humanity can only be understood to be a mere display of one of
his attributes. So, if the mercy of God is alone to be treated as a
'person' and that person is given the name of Jesus Christas , then
that something which died was the 'mercy' of God. What a
strange contradiction it is that the mercy of God, having taken
pity on sinful humanity, commits suicide. It implies that for three
days and nights there was no mercy left in God.

Remember that, in this scenario, Jesus[as] is not being treated as a
separate independent person, but only as a characteristic or an
aspect of God in which he becomes a sort of mercy personified.
That person, however, remains to be the one single indivisible
entity of God. So if anything died during this process, it would
have to be either the person God or the attribute of His Mercy,
which played the most vital role in this episode. Hence there is no
option but to believe in either the death of the Mercy of God, or
the death of Merciful God Himself.

Many complications would arise out of the claim that aspects of
a single person could be wiped out of existence, whether temporarily or permanently. This scenario can only be understood in
relation to its application to human experience. A man can lose

sight or hearing temporarily or permanently, but he would still be the same living man. The death of a faculty is, in fact, a partial death of the same person. In the ultimate analysis, the loser or sufferer remains the same individual entity.

Different Persons Sharing Eternity

If the elements of the Christian godhead were three different persons sharing eternity simultaneously, the question would arise as to their internal relationship. If they were eternally three persons making up one god, they have to have their own independent egos, so that the suffering of one, if he could suffer, would be his own personal experience. The others could sympathise with him, but could not actually participate in and share the suffering. Of course it is almost impossible to imagine the thought mechanism and decision-making processes of God, but the claim that He is actually three persons moulded into one justifies an effort to interrelate the three independent thought processes.

One possible scenario, which arises, is that of a human child born with three heads. This enormity can be referred to as a single person by virtue of there being only one trunk and four limbs, but three heads do present a problem of describing their true nature. If such freaks of nature live long enough to be able to speak and express themselves only then can we enquire as to what is happening inside the three different heads. In the absence of such knowledge, however, to declare them to be one person sharing three minds or three persons sharing one body is not possible.

It is strange that this very important aspect of Christian doctrine is not explained in the scriptures at all. As far as the reference to Christ[as] and the Holy Ghost is concerned there is no dearth of evidence that they are presented as two distinct persons, who did not share the same thought processes and the same feelings. Otherwise the visions of the Holy Ghost as distinct from Christ[as] would be impossible to conceive, particularly during the period that Christ[as] was confined to his human body.

The questions that would certainly arise as to what actually happened to the person of Christ[as] during that experience, in relation to the other two constituents of Christian Godhead, are:

1. Did the other two constituents, that is, God the Father and the Holy Ghost, jointly share in any way the body of Jesus Christ[as] or his experiences in their relation to that body?

2. Was Jesus[as] the sole occupant of that body and as such he did not share his experience in relation to that body with either of the remaining two constituents of the Trinity?

The ramifications of the former have already been discussed. In the case of the latter a further complication arises as to the relationship of Jesus[as], at that time, with the other two constituents of Trinity. Did Jesus[as] become a completely separate entity by himself during that period or did he remain an integral part of the other two constituents, only additionally occupying a dwelling in the form of a human body exclusively? Now we have another question to answer:

3. Was his divine entity entirely contained in his human body, or was it only projected out of the commonly shared form of God

the Father and the Holy Ghost like a tiny finger jutting out of an amoeba's body?

This scenario will also have us believe that during that phase Jesus[as] was greater than both his co-partners because he equally shared the form of existence with the Father and the Holy Ghost, while they did not share the jutted out finger of his human existence.

Hence, to make matters easily understandable, an attempt is made to illustrate the inherent paradoxes and absurdities by visualising different hypothetical situations. Of course, the illustrations should not be taken literally by the readers.

The issue before us is whether there is a single person exhibiting different attributes or going through different phases. This brings us to the question of considering the proposition of 'Three beings in One' and 'One being in Three', particularly from the angle of different phases as distinct from each other, and displaying different characters and moods by the same person.

This position has been considered at length in a previous chapter. Here, it is only necessary to re-emphasise the point that if one person or one entity exhibits different phases, it cannot exhibit those different phases simultaneously, without dividing itself into different parts.

Take, for example, water in a certain measure and quantity. It can be turned entirely into vapour or ice without compromising the singleness of its entity. If it is to be simultaneously observed in these different phases, it would have to be split so that a third of it would be ice, a third vapour and a third liquid. Each form would be different from the other, with none sharing the other two phases simultaneously. That quantity of water would be split into three states, but the size of each would certainly be smaller than the totality of the substance and no one can declare it to be 'One in Three' and 'Three in One'. Similarly, the incarnation of Christ[as] in the human form of Jesus[as], while keeping both the bondages between Jesus[as] the man and God the Father intact, is inconceivable.

All human beings are made up of the same elements, but their conformity and similarity to each other does not turn them into one single person. It is their characteristics, individualities and separateness from one another, which divides them into a multitude of entities, although they are intrinsically made from the same substance. One cannot, however, call them 'one in five billion' and 'five billion in one', despite their all sharing the humanity factor.

Let us now examine the same question from another angle. If, for any specific period of time, Jesus[as] was separate and distinguishable from God the Father on the one hand, and the Holy Ghost on the other, in which areas did that distinct separate existence of Christ[as] lie? Remember that one has to conceive of Christ[as] as being so totally distinct and disengaged from the Father and the Holy Ghost that his sacrifice for his fellow human brothers, or shall we say partial human brothers, must be thought of as entirely his own personal experience, different from that of the Father or the Holy Ghost This would evidently result in our considering Christ[as] alone transferring his mind or his thought processes to the physical body of Jesus[as]. Also then he could be understood as having undergone an experience, which was not shared by the other two components of the Christian Trinity. Mind boggling, is it not?

Different Persons with Distinctly Different Characters

If God the Father, Jesus[as] and the Holy Ghost were three persons with individual characters, not entirely shared by others, then they may not be considered as 'Three in One' and 'One in Three'. The complete merger of the Trinity into Unity can only be conceived if the characters, attributes, functions and all the faculties possessed by three persons become identical to each other's, without any distinctive feature separating one from the other.

This presents a scenario which could to a degree be likened to that of identical triplets, who with reference to their mind, heart, feelings and the functions of their organs are in such perfect unison that the individual experience of each of them is shared by the others completely. If this happens then something of the Trinity of God, the Son and the Holy Ghost could become more understandable. But the problem would still remain concerning the three bodies, which contain the three identical persons. This of course is not applicable to the Christian idea of Trinity. At second glance one is compelled to visualize a single body possessing three identities. Again, such an identity of the so-called triplets can only be visualized if one body can contain three persons, which in itself poses many problems. However, it can be pointed out that God has no body and as such the similitude of a human body, as suggested, is not applicable. Of course, we fully understand that God has no body in human terms, but the problem would still remain concerning three spiritual beings as identical triplets, individually as persons, yet being one in all other respects.

Another problem, which would confront the existence of hypothetical triplets would be their relationship with regards to worship. Would the 'Three in One' spiritual persons of the godhead worship one another? Would they all be the recipients of worship by their creation without there being any exercise of worship in relation to each other?

Although repeated mention is made in the New Testament of Jesus Christ[as] worshipping 'God the Father' and admonishing others to do the same, no such mention has been made in relation to the Holy Ghost worshipping God the Father. Again, there has never been any attempt by Jesus[as], as recorded in the New Testament, to exhort others to worship him or to worship the Holy Ghost One is intrigued by this total absence of reference to worship except in relation to God the Father.

Although it is a common practice among the Christians to worship Jesus[as] as the 'Son of God' along with the Father, there are no recorded instances of any of the disciples of Jesus Christ[as] ever having worshipped him or Jesus[as] prompting them to do so during his sojourn on Earth. Even if he had done so, it would raise many unanswerable questions. Again the same applies to the Holy Ghost and raises the question why did the Holy Ghost not require anyone to worship him.

The case where they were 'Three in One' in the sense that their ultimate ego or consciousness of existence was one, despite being divided into three aspects or phases, has already been examined at some length. A being of such a description cannot be logically referred to as 'three persons in one'. Moreover, aspects or phases are neither worshipped nor do they worship their own central ego. To conceive of these as separate persons they have to have their own independent identity in the form of an ultimate ego, which offers a reference point to their consciousness as persons. Otherwise the question of referring to themselves and others as 'I', 'You' and 'He', simply does not arise.

Trinity in application to one being can only be conceived as attributes and no more, and as far as attributes are concerned, they are certainly not limited to three. Whether we know them or not, God could possess a multitude of attributes.

To bring this discussion to a conclusion, we re-emphasise that the question of worship in relation to each other can only arise if they were different persons who did not enjoy equal status and equal characteristics.

In this instance, only one would be worthy of worship and the other two by the logic of their being inferior would be expected to worship him. The answer, again, is acceptable except that the 'Oneness in Trinity' will vanish. There is no way that you can have both 'Three in One' and 'One in Three' simultaneously.

This reminds me of a joke which I would like to share with you. It is reported that Joha, a famous court jester, so amused Tamerlane during his invasion of Baghdad that he decided to carry him back with him as booty and appointed him as the chief court jester. Once, it is said, Joha felt like eating meat alone by himself so much that he could not resist it any more. So he bought two kilos of the best meat available from the butcher. While handing it over to his wife he instructed her to prepare a delicious roast out of it, and that no one, including the wife, except him must touch it. Unfortunately for him, however, as his wife had just finished cooking, a few of her brothers gave her a surprise call. This was a pleasant surprise for her indeed but one which was destined to become a very unpleasant surprise for Joha. The tempting aroma of the freshly roasted meat was simply too much for them to resist and what followed was a logical conclusion. Having finished it to the last morsel they happily took leave of their rather worried sister. However, she had composed herself by the time Joha returned home and was ready with a foolproof excuse. When Joha, also smelling the remnant of the flavour, longingly asked for his two kilos of meat, the wife responded by pointing at the cat which was Joha's favourite pet, and said: 'Take your meat out of this cat, if you can. While I was busy working, he made short work of the entire roast' Thereupon Joha immediately picked the cat and weighed him in the scale. It so happened that the cat turned out to weigh exactly two kilos. Then he turned gently to his wife and enquired: 'Please my dear, I do believe you of course, but if this is my meat then where is my cat, and if this is my cat where is my meat!'

Jokes aside, let me assert that I do not wish to contend this issue on the basis of Jesus'[as] real and true teachings. This treatise is purely an exercise in viewing the current Christian doctrines which we believe have deviated a long way from the original teachings of Jesus[as].

Having denied that there is any reference in the Bible to Jesus[as] being worshipped, it is left to us to explain the only reference relating to this, in Luke 24:52[*]. Many claim that these verses provide evidence of Jesus[as] himself exhorting his followers to worship him. Contemporary Christian scholars are well aware that these verses have been proved to be spurious and have no right to be treated as a genuine part of St Luke's Gospel.

Let us now turn to the question of common practice, whether it is supported by evidence in the Gospels or not. According to the common practice, in many sects of Christianity today, Jesus[as] is indeed being worshipped as the 'Son of God'. Yet they all agree that the same Jesus[as] whom they worship used to worship God the Father and Him alone.

In vain I have often enquired from knowledgeable Christian scholars as to the reason why Jesus[as] should have worshipped God the Father if he himself was an inseparable part of God and was so completely merged with Him so as to create a sense of unity despite there being three persons? Did he ever worship the third constituent of the Trinity, that is the Holy Ghost? Did he ever worship himself? Did the Holy Ghost ever worship Jesus[as]? Did the Father ever worship either of the remaining two? If not, why? Perhaps the answer to these questions would compel the Christians to confess that a distinct superiority is certainly established of God the Father over the remaining two constituents of the

---

[*] The Bible translated by James Moffatt, published by Harper & Brothers, printed in the USA.

Trinity. From this it emerges that the three constituents of Trinity are not identical in their status. Hence they are 'Three in Three', if at all they are three, but they are not 'Three in One'. Sometimes when Christian scholars are confronted with the question of Jesus[as], whom they believe to be the Son of God, having worshipped God the Father, they claim that it was the man who worshipped God the Father, and not the Son Jesus[as] who did so. That takes us back to the discussion, which we have already covered earlier. Were there two conscious beings possessing the same body of Jesus[as], one possessing human consciousness and the other that of the Son of God?

Again, why did the man bypass and completely ignore the Son God in him and never worship Christ[as] as such? The same man Jesus[as], the co-partner of Christ[as], should also have worshipped the third constituent the Holy Ghost, which he never did.

Worship is an act of mind and soul that is expressed sometimes in bodily symbols, but it remains an act rooted in the mental and emotional entity of the person. Hence it has to be determined who worshipped when Jesus Christ[as] worshipped God. We have already dealt with the scenario, with all its intricacies, in which it is Christ[as], the Son of God, who worshipped. Conversely, if it was the man who worshipped God the Father and if he never worshipped Christ[as], then why on earth do the Christians defy this holy example of Jesus[as] himself? Why should they start worshipping Christ[as] beside God, while Jesus[as] the man never worshipped his co-partner Christ[as], despite being so close to him.

Different Persons with Identical and Equal Characters

Once again let us now examine, from a different angle this time, the formula of 'Three in One' in Trinity as three distinct persons who are absolutely and completely identical to each other. In this scenario we are not talking about a single person with different features combined in one but of three separate forms, rather like triplets. We refer to the kind of triplets, which are so completely identical that their similarities do not end with likeness of form alone, but also extend to the entire thinking and feeling processes. They share their thoughts, feelings and experiences identically. In this case one has to admit that two out of the three constituents of the Trinity are superfluous. If they are done away with, it will not in the least affect the remaining constituent of Trinity, which will remain complete in it.

The Holy Quran also raises the same question when it points out that if God decided to destroy and wipe out of existence both Jesus Christ[as] and the Holy Ghost, what difference will it make to His Majesty, Eternity and Perfection and who can stop Him from doing so (the Holy Quran 5:18). It implies that all the divine attributes will continue to function eternally and as such the concept of the Trinity as portrayed in this scenario appears senseless and needless.

If, however it is supposed that the three distinct persons in the Trinity perform different functions, then obviously all three components would become essential to the making of the God-head. Nevertheless, in this case there will be three distinct Gods cooperating with each other and living together in perfect harmony and as such they can only be treated as 'Three Gods in Three' and not 'Three Gods in One'.

Again if it is proposed that the Trinity is similar to the case of a single person with different organic functions, all combined in one, then of course Unity can be retained but not Trinity. Here we are not discussing a person with different organic functions but three entirely identical persons, each performing similar functions yet retaining its individuality. What is being discussed presents the case of a single person with different organs. So far there is nothing illogical about it. But when the organs are treated as persons in their own right and at the same time they are believed to constitute a personality which in its totality is one, then the confines of logic are breached and the whole discussion becomes unacceptable. Indeed organs have their individuality, but their individuality is only a component of a larger personality, which not only comprises this one organ but also other organs. All such organs together within a man are called 'man' in its totality. Of course some organs perform relatively minor functions and man can remain a man without them, but only with imperfection. A perfect man must possess all organs that are commonly possessed by a human being and the sum total of these organs would make him a perfect man.

If we take the case of a man called Paul, one cannot say that since the liver, heart, lungs and kidneys of Paul have individuality with specific functions to perform, they are distinct persons completely identifiable with Paul. Complete identification can only be possible if, say, the kidneys function exactly like Paul in his totality and the same can be said of his other organs. That proposition would require that the absence of each organ would not change the character of Paul in any manner or alternatively Paul even without his lungs, heart, kidneys and brain, indeed with all his organs removed, would still remain a complete Paul in himself. This is because in the ultimate analysis they are all exactly similar to each other and the person of Paul remains absolutely intact, irrespective of the absence of these organs.

If that is the scenario of 'Three in One' then of course it is wrong to make any attempts to criticize Christian beliefs with reference to logic. Then the logic, which is applicable to the present day Christian dogma, is only the logic of the witches of Macbeth when they say: 'Fair is foul, and foul is fair'.

CHAPTER SEVEN

THE EVOLUTION OF CHRISTIANITY

THE DOCTRINE OF TRINITY, which is one of the fundamental constituents of Christian dogma, was absent from Christianity during the lifetime of Jesus Christ[as]. The maximum one can grant is that this doctrine started taking shape after the Crucifixion. It took many centuries for it to reach its final well defined but inexplicable form. It went through a long process of extremely bitter and controversial debates between Christian theologians and philosophers representing different religious, cultural and traditional backgrounds.

It was greatly influenced by the myths and the traditions of various lands, which hosted Christianity in its early period. The main stem of Christianity, however, which took care of and nurtured the development of Christian beliefs and philosophy in its early formative part was of Jewish stock. Jewish influence remained predominant throughout the early part of Christian history. The disciples of Jesus[as], who learnt and understood Christianity directly from Jesus[as] and witnessed it in the form of his life, belonged to this stock. They were the primary custodians of Christianity and had deeply embedded roots in the holy soil of Jesus'[as] instructions and way of life. It was they who witnessed the Crucifixion and had seen Jesus[as] survive from his attempted murder.

The First Followers of Jesus

Early Christians appear to have been fundamentally divided over both the nature of Jesus[as] and whether to adhere to the Mosaic Law or not. In the second phase of Christian development, St Paul acquired the most pivotal character in giving Christianity a new philosophy and ideology. There were fundamental differences of opinion between Paul and James the Righteous. While James looked after the Jerusalem Church, Paul was preaching in the West, particularly to the gentiles. The Western Church evolved along Pauline doctrinal lines, whereas the Church in Jerusalem developed along monotheistic teachings.

One offshoot of James' ministry was the Ebionites, a sect whose name derives from the Hebrew *ebionim* meaning 'the meek' or 'the poor'. They were the Jewish Christians, for whom Jesus[as] took on the mantle of Messiah and not that of the 'Son of God'.

They followed the Mosaic law with great zeal, and had their own Gospel known in various contexts as the 'Gospel of the Hebrews', 'Gospel of the Ebionites' or the 'Gospel of the Nazarenes'. Here is a description of the Ebionites drawn from various sources.

In his book '*The History of the Church*' written in the 4th century AD in Caesarea, Eusebius mentions the Ebionites in Book 3, *Vespasian to Trajan*. He mocks at their views, saying that their name comes from their poor and mean opinion of Jesus[as]. The Ebionites regarded Jesus[as] as mortal and esteemed him as righteous through the growth of his character. As Jews, they observed the Sabbath, and every detail of the Law, and did not accept the

Pauline idea of salvation through faith alone. He also talks of another group of Ebionites who accepted the virgin birth and the Holy Spirit, but refused to accept Jesus'[as] pre-existence as 'God the Word and Wisdom'. They followed a 'Gospel of the Hebrews' which could possibly have been St Matthew's Gospel. They observed the Sabbath and Jewish system, but celebrated the resurrection.[*]

R. Eisenman and M. Wise while describing the background of Ebionites in their book *The Dead Sea Scrolls Uncovered* (1992) say that James (the 'Zaddik' or 'Zadok', meaning Righteous) was the leader of the Jerusalem Church in the middle of the first century (40–60 AD approx.). The branch was retrospectively called *Jewish Christianity* in Palestine. The Ebionites developed from this branch.[*]

The Community who followed James were known as 'the Poor', (Galatians 2:10, James 2:3–5) a designation mentioned both in the Sermon on the Mount and in the *Dead Sea Scrolls*. In many ways, Eisenman feels that the Ebionites were similar to the authors of *the Dead Sea Scrolls*. They honoured James the Righteous, and believed Jesus[as] to be their mortal Messiah, while Paul had become an *Apostate for the Law*. They observed the Law and

---

[*] 'The Dead Sea Scrolls Uncovered,' R Eisenman and M Wise, p. 186, (Element Books, 1992)
[*] 'The Dead Sea Scrolls Uncovered,' R Eisenman and M Wise, p. 233-234, (Element Books, 1992)

the Sabbath with great zeal. They held James in the highest regard, while Paul was considered 'The Enemy'.[*]

According to Baigent, Leigh and Lincoln in *The Messianic Legacy*, the source of the original teachings of the Ebionites, Gnostics, Manicheans, Sabians, Mandeans, Nestorians and Elkasites has been described as the Nazarene philosophy. They refer to Nazarene thought as:

'An orientation towards Jesus and his teachings which derives ultimately from the original Nazarene position, as articulated by Jesus himself, then propagated by James, Jude or Judas Thomas and their immediate entourage.' Their beliefs were:

1. *Strict adherence to the Mosaic Law*
2. *Recognition of Jesus as Messiah*
3. *Belief in the normal human birth of Jesus*
4. *Hostility towards Pauline views*

There is a collection of Arabic manuscripts kept in a library in Istanbul which contains quotes from a 5th or 6th Century text ascribed to the 'Al-Nasara', written in Syriac and found in a monastery in Khuzistan in south-west Iran near the Iraq border. It reflects the views of the Nazarene hierarchy escaping from Jerusalem after the destruction in 66 AD. It refers to Jesus as a human being and stresses the Judaic Law.

---

[*] 'The Messianic Legacy'. M Baigent, R Leigh, H Lincoln, p. 135-138 (Corgi Books)

*Paul's followers abandoned the religion of Christ and turned towards the religious doctrines of the Romans.**

Of all the various doctrines which evolved during the formative stages of Christianity, only those who believed in the Nazarene philosophy can justifiably be given preference. These early Christians were taught the meaning of Christianity by Jesus[as] himself.

The Role of St Paul

Evidently St Paul and his school do not belong there. In fact, from the time of St Paul onwards, as Christianity spread to alien lands and pagan faiths within the Roman Empire, it began to be powerfully influenced and bent by the cultures and mythologies prevalent in those lands and went further away from its nascent purity. St Paul did his bit in influencing the deterioration of the Christian thought by introducing his own brand of mysticism. He was neither of Jewish stocks nor did he have any direct contact with Jesus[as], except through his claimed vision. He was already, it seems, under the powerful influence of the alien cultures.

Apparently there were two options available to St Paul, either to fight strenuous battles against a world of superstitions, myths and legends prevalent in the lands of the Roman Empire from times immemorial or to give in to them and let Christianity change to suit their requirements and ambitions. This gave them

---

* 'The Hiram Key'. Christopher Knight and Robert Lomas, p. 246 (Century 1996)

the message that Christianity was not essentially different from their legends and myths. He found the adoption of the second option far more profitable and convenient and let Christianity change to suit the ambitions and philosophies popular in the gentile world. This strategy worked well in as much as it gained a great number of converts to the new faith who otherwise would not have been easily available. But at what cost? Unfortunately, it ended up only in an unholy competition between noble Christian values and pagan myths. What St Paul changed was only the names of the pagan gods and replaced them with Jesus[as], God the Father and the Holy Ghost. It was not him in fact who invented the myth of Trinity and introduced it to the pagan world in the name of Christianity, on the contrary, he borrowed the myth of the Trinity from pagan mythology and bonded it to Christianity. From then on it was the same old paganism but with new names and new faces.

Pauline Christianity, therefore, did not succeed in changing the doctrines, myths and superstitions of the pagan world but only ended in changing Christianity in accordance with them. If the mountain did not respond to his call, he decided to go to the mountain.

The Reality of Jesus

Of course it is anybody's prerogative to choose between Pauline Christianity and that of James the Righteous and other early leaders of Christianity who were the disciples of Jesus Christ[as] himself. But here we want to establish the point that the main stock of Christianity continued to develop along unitarian lines and kept itself aloof from the later innovations which generated the rigmarole and complexities of Christian dogmas such as the godhead of Jesus[as] as the Son, the Trinity, Inherited Sin, Redemption, physical revival of Jesus[as], etc. The views of the early leaders of the Church, among whom James the Righteous is prominent, were simple and honest and had no internal contradictions or paradoxes hiding behind a smoke screen of mystery. A study of the history of Unitarianism in Christianity establishes beyond question the fact that the Unity of God, uncomplicated by the slogan of Trinity, remained the official doctrine of the true Church of Christ[as] in its pristine purity.

Please remember that this short treatise is not an attempt to convert Christians to any faith other than that of Christ[as]. It is simply a genuine effort to invite the Christians back to the pure unadulterated faith and practice of Jesus[as] himself. It is a sincere attempt to revert the fiction back to the facts of Christianity— facts that are certainly as beautiful as they are realistic and satisfy both the head and the heart.

For almost two thousand years, it is not the legends woven around the reality of Jesus Christ[as] that have kept Christianity together and have helped it to survive the challenges of reason and ever growing enlightenment borne out of scientific progress, nor is its survival due to the mystic belief of Trinity. What has held the truth and essence of Christianity together is the beauty of the person and the teachings of Jesus Christ[as]. It is the divine conduct and not the divine person of Jesus[as] that has been so beautiful to adhere to. It was the suffering, patience and perseverance for the sake of noble ideals and his bold upright rejection of all despotic attempts to make him change his principles that have been the real backbone of Christianity. It is still as beautiful and as loveable today as it was ever before. It has influenced so powerfully the Christian minds and hearts that they remain bonded to Jesus[as] and would much rather shut their eyes to logical discrepancies than to break away from him.

His real greatness lies in the fact that he transcended and conquered the forces of darkness that had conspired to vanquish him despite being a frail human being and no more than a human being. That victory of Jesus[as] is something to be shared with pride by the children of Adam[as]. As we see it from the Muslim vantage point, he is one of the most noble progeny of Adam[as]. He taught humanity by his example of perseverance in the face of extreme suffering and pain. Not to surrender but to remain steadfast in the teeth of extreme trial was the noblest achievement of Jesus[as]. It was his life of suffering and pain that redeemed humanity and made him conquer death. If he had accepted death voluntarily, it would have been tantamount to an attempt to escape his state of suffering. How can one conceive this to be an act of bravery? Even the act of those who commit suicide, under extreme pressure, is taken to be a mere act of cowardice. To share suffering in life is far better than to escape suffering through death. Hence the concept of the supreme sacrifice of Jesus[as] by accepting death for the sake of humanity is hollow sentimentality with no substance in it.

The greatness of Jesus[as], we again insist, lay in his supreme sacrifice during his lifetime. All his life, he defied the temptations to give in and exchange a life of suffering with that of ease and comfort. Day in, day out he confronted death but refused to give in and lived for the sake of the sinful to bring them to life. He conquered death not by surrendering himself to death, but by refusing to bow down to it. He defeated it roundly and emerged from its clutches where a lesser man would have perished. Thus he proved his truth and the truth of his word beyond a shadow of doubt. That is how we see Jesus[as] and that is why we love him so. His voice was the voice of God and not the voice of his own ambitions. He said what he was commissioned to say, neither more nor less than what God had told him to say. He worshipped God throughout his life and worshipped Him alone and never did he require any mortal to bow before him or before his mother or the Holy Ghost. This is the reality of Jesus[as] to which we invite the Christians of all denominations and faiths to return.

The Continuity of Religion

We believe in the continuity and universality of religions. That is why Islam lays such emphasis on the institution of Prophethood as a universal phenomenon, which means that Prophets[as] have to be accepted in their totality. Rejection of one out of the community of Prophets[as] would be tantamount to rejection of all because, in fact, one bows to the Prophets[as] only in view of their hailing from the same source. In this context, the term 'continuity' should be understood as something that is similar but not exactly like the evolution of life. We believe in the progressiveness of the message, advancing in step with general human progress in all spheres of human activity. It appears that the earlier forms of revealed religions, though possessing the same fundamental teachings, covered relatively smaller areas of detailed instruction. That is to say, a smaller number of do's and don'ts. These then gradually grew into a larger number of imperatives and prohibitions covering a wider field of human activity. Also, it appears that religions belonging to the ancient civilizations addressed themselves to comparatively smaller audience belonging to particular tribes, or clans or regions. Their messages were confined to the requirements of the time. They could be more aptly described as tribal, clannish or national religions. The case of the Children of Israel and Judaic teachings is a fitting illustration to prove the point.

The historic trend of development, therefore, can be summarised as two-fold: A progressive elaboration and comparative perfection of the teachings; a progressive shift from smaller to larger denominations.

Continuity does not mean that the same religion that was revealed to Adam continued to address mankind and underwent a gradual progressive change, widening its field of instruction and address. What is meant is that in different parts of the world, where different civilizations took root and flourished, Divine revelations gave birth to such religions with corresponding social developments of man in those parts of the world. All of these religions, however, were developing in the same general direction.

The Apex of Religious Development

Of all such religious denominations, we believe the one in the Middle East was being nurtured and cultured to give birth to such major religions as would serve the main stem of religious evolution in the world. This is quite evident from a study of religious history. Judaism followed by Christianity followed by Islam, clearly indicates the direction of the evolution of religious teachings. Among these religions, the progression of teachings can easily be traced back and forth and is found to be deeply interrelated. It is highly important, therefore, to understand this grand scheme of things which was to result and did result in the consummation of these teachings in the form of a universal religion, that is Islam.

In this context it is in the interest of the Jews to seriously and without prejudice try to understand the importance of Jesus Christ[as]. Having failed to recognise him, the case of the Jews is like that of so many animal species buried deep in the history of evolution, which are no longer playing any vital role in the evolving tree of life nearing its summit. As such, it remains only as a remnant of history but still continuing to survive in its own narrow sphere of existence.

Again the case of the Christians is similar to that of the Jews, only they stand a step ahead of them, closer to Islam in the chronological order. Most importantly, however, those deviations from the path of Jesus Christ[as] into a decadent course which was originally set for them by St Paul has virtually led them even farther away from Islam than the Jews. The Jews, after more than four thousand years of their existence, have at least learnt the lesson of Unity which is vital for the spiritual life of any religion. Yet despite this closeness to Islam in the basic doctrines, there are other factors which make the Jews even more adamant in refusing to accept Islam in large numbers.

This study leaves me to believe that unless the Jews develop that frame of mind and attitude which is a requisite for the understanding of Christ[as], despite their doctrinal similarities, they will remain farther apart from Islam than the Christians. They have missed a most vital link, that is Jesus Christ[as], between them and the advent of Prophet Muhammad[sa]. This denial of truth has hardened them to such a degree that they are not psychologically prepared to accept any new message. They continue to wait for Christ[as], while Christ[as] has come and gone. Having failed to recognise him once, they are far less likely to recognise him again during his second advent. They are destined, it seems, to be waiting for the Christ[as] of their dreams eternally.

It was Christ[as] who was to prepare the pathway to the following higher order religion which is Islam. This statement should not be taken too rigidly. We are not suggesting that the Jews should first accept Christianity and then take the next step into Islam. It would be too naive a view of religious manifestations as they take place. What we are trying to point out is that a people who have rejected a Prophet[as] or a Messenger[as], who was not just an ordinary Prophet[as] but was to play a very important role in the task of the mental and spiritual training of that people, do so only when they are spiritually and psychologically ill. Unless this malady is cured and that distorted attitude towards truth is rectified, they are less likely to follow a Prophet who happens to be placed beyond the link they have already missed.

As far as the Christian attitude is concerned, they can only be led to the truth of Prophet Muhammad[sa] if they return to the truth and reality of Jesus Christ[as]. He was not only the way to God, but also like all the other Prophets was the way to the Prophet who was destined to follow him.

Jesus[as] was only the middle link in the parable of the vineyard. The last consummate representation of God was yet to come. Therefore, unless the Christians return from the false, imaginary and mythical image of Jesus Christ[as] to the much loftier and nobler reality of their holy master, they cannot be directed on to the path that connected him with Prophet Muhammad[sa].

Prophet Muhammad[sa] was a reality and not a fiction and it is only realities which lead to other realities. Therefore, it would be the fact of Christ[as], rather than the fiction he has been turned into, which would bless Christians to recognise the truth of Prophet Muhammad[sa].

CHAPTER EIGHT

CHRISTIANITY TODAY

THE GREATEST PROBLEM WHICH CONFRONTS the world of Christianity today is not lack of understanding as much as the lack of desire and will to accept truth. Christianity, whether it is mythical or factual, has become an inseparable part of Western civilization and has played an important role in their colonization and imperial conquests. It supports their political and economic systems and provides them with a unifying and coherent force that keeps them as one powerful and unified entity. It has played a vital role in building and cementing the complex socio-political and economic system of the West What we understand by Western civilization or Western Imperialism and its economic domination has all been pervaded with some Christian elements. In its present state, Christianity seems to be inclined to serve material causes of the West better than its spiritual cause. While in the past the role of Christianity was more in the direction of supporting Christian beliefs and building moral values.

The most historic role played by Christianity, however, lies in building and enhancing Western Imperialism. The Orient was conquered with Christian fervour and in particular the battles fought with the Muslim empire were strongly motivated by the Christian hatred of Islam.

Christianity and Colonialism

When colonial rule subjugated almost the entire continent of America and tied Africans from crown to toe in the chains of political bondage, they did not have to wait long until they were bound, hand and foot, in the chains of economic slavery as well. Imperial conquests are meaningless without an economic subjugation of the people. Not far behind the political and economic lords came the Christian priests, robed in humility and self-sacrifice. Their purpose to visit Africa appeared to be diametrically opposed to that of their political and economic vanguard. They came not to enslave, so they said, but to liberate the souls of Africa. It is surprising that the Africans did not question this purportedly noble intention. Why did they not respectfully enquire of the benign philanthropic leaders of the Church, as to why should they take pity on their souls and their souls alone? Could they not see how mercilessly their bodies had been enslaved? How wantonly had they been robbed of their political freedom? How they were bound in the chains of economic slavery? Why did they not take pity on their physical state of captivity and why were they only interested in liberating the souls of an enslaved people?

The inherent contradiction is obvious, but alas it was not so obvious to those who fell prey to the Christian designs. Africa is naive indeed, and as much naive today as it was two hundred years ago. Africans still do not see the perpetration of their political and economic slavery through the invisible, remote controlled system of neo-colonialism. They still do not realize that for them

Christianity is only a means of subjugation. It is like an opiate that has lulled them into a deep sleep of forgetfulness. It gives them a false sense of belonging to their rulers in sharing at least something on equal footing with them. It is the same sense of belonging which has led them to imitate the so expensive style of Western life. The trees remain planted on foreign soils, but only the fruits are transported across to a people who have somehow become addicted to their taste. This is a small illustration of how Christianity has always been indispensable for the Western imperial and economic domination of the Third World.

In the West itself, regardless of whether a common man understands the complexities of Christian dogma or not, he sees Christianity as an integral part of his culture and civilization. It should be remembered that the real strength of Christian values, wherever they survive, does not lie in Christianity's mythical set of beliefs. But instead it lies in the emphasis on kindness, sympathy, service to the cause of suffering and other such values that have almost become synonymous with Christianity. Although these values are common to all religions of the world and they seem to be the goal Divinely set to be attained by all humanity, yet somehow, the powerful Christian propaganda continuously emphasises these roles in relation to Christianity alone and, as such, has succeeded in convincing people at large. This message of sympathy, kindness, godliness and gentle behaviour plays magic to ears with its mellow music. It is this world of romance which generally attracts people to the Christian faith. However, side by side, yet divorced from it operate the hard, political and economic realities of Western life and its subjugation of the rest of the world.

It seems that the dogmatic paradoxes that the Christians have to live with have somehow been transferred into their worldly behaviour as well. Kindness, humility, tolerance, sacrifice and many other such noble words go hand in hand with cruelty, suppression, gross injustice and large scale subjugation of the defenceless peoples of the world. Rule of law, justice and fair play seem only to be valid currencies operable internally in the Western cultures. In the area of international relationships, however, they are treated as stupid and in obsolete terms to be taken seriously only by the naive.

International politics, diplomacy and economic relationships know no justice other than that which serves the national interest Christian values, however good they may be, are not permitted to step across into the domain of Western politics and economy. This is the most tragic contradiction of modern times.

When it comes to the image that it projects, Christianity is only presented in the form of an attractive Western culture and civilization calling the world of the Orient to a life of comfortable carefree permissiveness in comparison to the generally rigid codes of their decadent religious societies. This message of emancipation is largely misunderstood by the semi-literate masses of the Third World as something very attractive. Add to this the additional psychological advantage of acquiring a sense of belonging to the advanced world through the commonness of religion and then one begins to recognise the true role of Christianity in attracting in large numbers the downtrodden and, in many cases, outcast and oppressed people who are at the lowest rungs within their own class-ridden societies. It is beyond their power to understand

Christian dogma. It only serves to lift their human status, but spuriously so.

From the above it should become evident that the Christianity we are talking about is very distant from the Christianity of Jesus Christ[as]. To conceive of Western culture as Christianity is a manifest error. To attribute the current form of Christianity, in its various spheres, to Christ[as] is indeed an insult to him. There are exceptions of course to every rule. No statement is applicable in absolute totality to any group of large numbers. No doubt, there is a small number of individual islands of hope and life in the Christian world where Christian sincerity, love and sacrifice are genuinely practised. These are the islands of hope around which rage oceans of immorality that are slowly and gradually corroding and finally claiming more edges of these islands. Had the Christian world not been bejewelled with such shining examples of Christianity practised in the spirit of Jesus Christ[as], however few and far between, a total darkness would envelop the Western horizon. Without Christianity there is no light in Western civilization, but, alas, that light is also fast fading.

It is essential for the Christian world to return to the reality of Christ[as] and to cure themselves of their split identity and inherent hypocrisy. To continue to live in a world of myths and legends is potent with grave perils. The main purpose of this exercise is to awaken the Christian world to the potential dangers attendant upon the widening parallax between their belief and practice. Myths are fine as long as they serve the purpose of subjugating the lowest rungs of the society to the hierarchy of a system which controls them and exploits their ignorance by keeping them doped. But when it comes to the beliefs playing a vital role in bringing a dead people to life and reconstructing their fast degenerating moral values, then such myths are of no avail. They are mere fantasies and fantasies can never play a meaningful role in human affairs.

The Re-Advent of Jesus Christ

The application of the observations made so far can now be demonstrated. The vital question of the survival of humanity today, revolves around the central image of Jesus Christ[as]. It is highly essential, therefore, to understand his reality. What was he and what role did he play in the first instance as Christ[as] in the decadent society of Judaism? How seriously can we take the promise of his second advent in the latter days? These are the vital questions we must address.

If the image of Jesus Christ[as] is not real and is only a product of human imagination, then it is impossible to visualize his re-advent. Jesus[as], however, was not a product of fantasy. He was a real man and only as such could he be reborn as a human child and not descend as a phantom revisiting mortals. Such fantasies never visit the realities of human life. Moreover, a people who live with myths and legends continue to do so without there ever being a chance for them to recognise their redeemer, if and when he comes.

If Jesus[as] was actually the Son of God, as the Christians would have us believe, then of course he would return in glory, resting his hands on the shoulders of real angels. But if this is merely a romantic fantasy of Christian hopes and aspirations then, as such, this incident will never happen. Never shall the world see this bizarre event of some god descending from heaven in human form along with a troop of angels supporting him and singing his hymns.

The very idea is repulsive to human logic and human conscience. It is the wildest fairy tale that was ever invented to lull the faculties of a people. On the other hand if the Aḥmadiyya understanding of Jesus Christ^{as} is accepted, it would replace this fantastic scenario with one which is not only acceptable to human understanding, but is also powerfully supported by the entire religious history of mankind. In that case we would be expecting a saviour no different from the Christ^{as} of the first advent. We would be expecting a humble man, born of humble origins like Jesus Christ^{as} of the first advent, to begin his ministry in the same style as he once did. He would belong to a religious people resembling the Jews of Judea, both in their traits and circumstances. They would not only reject and disown him at his claim to be the Promised Reformer, which they were expecting as their redeemer from God, but would also do all that lay within their powers to annihilate him. He would relive the life of Christ^{as} all over again and would be treated with the same contempt, hatred and arrogance. He would suffer once again, not at the hands of his own people, but at the hands of hostile forces similar to those which opposed him before. He would also suffer at the hands of the supreme foreign imperial power under whose canopy he would be born among an enslaved people.

P.D. Ouspensky, a prominent Russian journalist of the early twentieth century, writing on the subject of the re-advent of Jesus Christ[as] shared almost the same view.

It is by no means a new idea that Christ[as], if born on earth later, not only could not be the head of the Christian Church, but probably would not even belong to it, and in the most brilliant periods of the might and power of the Church would most certainly have been declared a heretic and burned at the stake. Even in our more enlightened times, when the Christian Churches, if they have not lost their anti-Christian features, have at any rate begun to conceal them, Christ[as] could have lived without suffering the persecution of the 'scribes and Pharisees' perhaps only somewhere in a Russian hermitage.[*]

This is the only real process by which divine messengers and reformers are raised. Any concept other than this is hollow, spurious and meaningless.

It always happens that at a time when the prophetic fulfilment of prophecies about the advent of Divine reformers takes place, the people for whose redemption they are sent fail to recognise him. In that period of history they have already transformed the image of their reformer from reality to fantasy. They begin to expect a fantasy to appear and materialize, while what happens is

---

[*] P.D. Ouspensky, 'A New Model of the Universe', p. 149-150, Kegan Paul, Trench, Trubener & Co., Ltd 1938

merely a re-enacting of the religious history as it invariably occurred from the time of the first divine reformer. Reformers always appear as humble human beings born of human mothers and during their lifetime are always treated as humans. It is much later after their death that the process of their deification begins. As such, their smooth acceptance during their re-visit becomes impossible.

When such religious people are confronted with the realities of the divine reformers, who always appear as ordinary humble human beings, they reject them outright. When you are expecting a fairy to come or a phantom to materialize, how can you accept the coming of an ordinary human instead? That is the reason why the world failed to see and recognise the second advent of Jesus Christ[as], which has already taken place.

This is a tall claim perhaps, which is likely to be simply rejected by most readers. How could Jesus[as] have come and gone without the world having taken a serious note of it? How could he have gone unnoticed by the entire world of Christianity and Islam? The modern times have seen many such claimants who even created momentary stirs and storms in many a cup, but where are they today?

It is an age where in many countries, cults erupt like mushrooms and bizarre claims of Jesus[as] having returned or having sent his forerunner are made sporadically. This claim could perhaps be just one of those. Why should any serious minded person waste his time to even contemplate this? Certainly, serious doubts would be created and a grave dilemma would indeed be faced. We seek to indulge the reader's attention by requesting him to visualize a situation where Christ^{as} would actually have come. Is his revisit just a fantasy or can he really revisit the world in person or through proxy? This is a question, which has to be resolved before we can attempt to answer the various doubts mentioned above.

Is the world, be it Christian or Muslim, really in a psychological state of mind to accept the second advent of Jesus^{as}? If so, in what form and in which way? If we see it from the vantage point of both Muslims and the Christians, Jesus^{as}, if he were to ever return, would come with such glory and clear signs, descending from the heavens in broad daylight with angels supporting him, that it would be impossible for even the most sceptical to refuse to accept him.

Sadly, only a Jesus^{as} of fantasy is acceptable to the world of to-day, a Jesus^{as} the like of whom never came before in all of human history. If religious history is to be taken seriously, one finds scores of instances in which founders of religions or other divines are reported to have ascended to heaven bodily. These claims are so numerous and so widespread that it seems to be a universal trend of man to concoct such stories in order to elevate and super-humanise his religious leaders. The question is how can we deny all these reporting which are accepted and believed by perhaps billions of people in the world today? The Christians and Muslims alone who believe in this and other similar bizarre events number beyond two billion. So a reader may enquire as to what right we, or anyone else in the world, have to reject all such beliefs as unreal and imaginary. We agree that examining it from this angle will require a ponderous exercise to refute such claims as being unsupported by the scriptures of the religions, which entertain them. Once one is led into this maze of possible and alternative interpretations, it ends up only as a question of preferences and choices. It then becomes anybody's game to interpret scriptures or reported religious history as literal or metaphorical. To step into this quagmire of conflicting explanations would serve no purpose. Yet there is one exit from this onerous exercise that we can show readers and invite them to follow or reject as they please.

For argument's sake let us accept all such claims of religious leaders having ascended to heaven and take them at their face value. If the case of Jesus Christ's[as] reported ascent is to be treated in a superficial sense and his second coming to be interpreted as literal and real, then there is no reason why we should refuse to accept other similar cases in the world. Why make an exception of Elijah; King of Salem; the Twelfth Imam of the Shiite faction in Islam; the ascension of Hindu gods; or other similar holy men and the so-called personifications of God? It is safer, therefore, to avoid entering into such unproductive, futile debates with those who entertain such beliefs. One may enquire, from all such credulous believers in fantasy if they can point out a single revisit, in person, of those who are reported to have disappeared by ascending into remote heavenly recesses. Can all of human history present a single example of the bodily return of any person to this world who is reported to have bodily ascended? Show us if there is one.

Looking at the total absence of literal fulfilment of such claims, one is left with two choices: either to reject such claims as fraudulent, or accept them only metaphorically, as Jesus[as] did in the case of Elijah's second coming. It becomes evident from this that those who await Jesus'[as] literal descent from heaven have created a barrier between themselves and the reality of Jesus[as]. If Jesus[as] comes again he will come only as a human being just like all the expected divine reformers before him. If he appears today as an ordinary humble person, having been born in a land similar to the land of Judea in Palestine and commissioned to play the same role he played during his first advent, will the people of that land treat him in a manner other than he was treated before?

The Promised Messiah

Such is the case of the second advent of the Messiah[as] in whom we believe. It happened just over a hundred years ago that a humble man of God, by the name of Mirza Ghulam Ahmad of Qadian was informed by God that Jesus[as] of Nazareth, Son of Mary[as], whose literal second coming is being awaited both by the Christians and the Muslims alike, was a special Prophet of God who passed away like all other prophets of God. Hadrat Mirza Ghulam Ahmad[as] declared that Jesus[as] was not bodily alive and was never bodily lifted to any heavenly space to await his revisit to this earth. He had died like all other Prophets of God and was no more than a Prophet. The second advent of Jesus Christ[as], a belief common to Christians and Muslims alike, he was told, was to take place spiritually and not literally. As such, he was told that God had raised him in the fulfilment of that prophecy.

Mirza Ghulam Aḥmad belonged to a noble family of the Punjab. His family's pursuits were mostly concerned with building their fortune and honour, but he distanced himself from worldly pursuits and spent most of his time in the worship of God and religious studies. He was a man almost lost to the world, little known even in the small township of his birth. Then slowly he began to emerge on the religious horizon of India as a stalwart and a champion of the cause of Islam. He became known as a holy man of such fame that he commanded respect not only among Muslims, but also from the followers of other religions. People began to witness in him a man in communion with God, whose prayers were answered, whose deep sincere concern for humanity and the suffering of people was beyond question.

Islam, during this period in India, was unfortunately in a most pitiful state. It was targeted by the Christian missionaries, who in accordance with the policies of the British Empire, launched a vitriolic campaign not only against Islamic teachings but also against the Holy Founder[sa] of Islam. Also, in Hinduism, the major religion of India, extremely ambitious movements were taking form with a two pronged plan: to revive Hindu culture and practice and to eliminate Islam and the Muslims from India, portraying them as aliens having no right to remain rooted on its soil. The most aggressive among these was the Ārya Samāj Movement, which was founded by Pandit Swāmī Dyānand Sarsūtī (1824–1883) in 1875. This perhaps further motivated Ḥaḍrat Mirza Ghulam Aḥmad to begin extensive research in comparative religions in defence of Islam.

His studies further strengthened his belief in the superiority of the teachings of Islam. He was impressed by the distinctive approach of the Holy Quran to human problems. The Holy Quran, he discovered, after presenting a course of human conduct did not stop at that instruction arbitrarily, but continued to build strong, logical arguments supported by evidence that the prescribed course was the most appropriate option in the given context.

His studies enabled him, at last, to champion the cause of Islam, which at that time was practically defenceless. Thus he performed the most pressing requirement for the defence of Islam in India at that period. He began his public life by holding dialogues and debates on a smaller scale which gradually expanded into much wider circles. His fame as the most competent and formidable proponent for the cause of Islam began to spread far and wide.

It was in that period of time that he commenced the authoring of one of the greatest literary religious works that he ever undertook. This book, *Brāhīn-e-Ahmadiyya*, was planned to be published in fifty volumes but he could only publish the first five while tumultuous events overtook him and from then on it was no longer possible for him to pursue that scholarly task to its conclusion. However, he subsequently authored many other books in response to the dictates of the time. His books covered almost the entire subject which he had originally intended to cover and much more. In fact he did more than fulfil his promise though not under the title. It is amazing how he could produce such vast literature almost single-handedly, without much clerical help. The books, epistles and treatises which he authored number around one hundred and ten.[*]

It was not just his literary works that won him such wide recognition in the entire sub-continent but also his spiritual qualities played a vital role in winning him wide-scale fame and respect.

In this twilight of his rising and widening reputation he was commissioned by God to bear the grave responsibility of being the Reformer of the latter days who was expected and awaited by almost all religions of the world. From the Muslims' point of view he was Al-Mahdi[as], the divinely guided reformer. From the viewpoint of both the Christians and the Muslims he was raised to the status of the Promised Messiah[as] to fulfil the prophecies of the second advent of Jesus Christ[as]. However, this appointment cost him all the fame and popularity that he had earned previously. Hadrat Mirza Ghulam Ahmad, the divinely appointed spiritual reformer of the age, was abandoned forthwith and rejected not only by the followers of other faiths but more strongly so by the Muslims of India themselves, the people whose cause he had been so competently and vehemently pleading.

It was practically a new spiritual birth for him. As he had come alone to the world so he was to start a new life as a single man in the world of religion, practically abandoned by all around him. But God did not abandon him. He was repeatedly assured by

---

[5] This count does not includes the number of letters which he wrote to his followers and others and which run into thousands (Publisher)

God's succour and support through different revelations that he received during the period of intense hostility. At another time it was revealed:

"A warner came into the world but was not accepted, but God will accept him and will establish his truth with mighty signs."

"I shall spread thy message to the ends of the earth."

These are some of the early revelations, which helped him to sustain during the state of utter desolation and rejection he suffered at the hands of his opponents. More than a hundred years have passed since and the picture that has slowly but steadily emerged fully supports his claims and prophecies and the truth of his revelations.

That one man has grown into ten million people all over the world in a hundred and thirty four countries spread over five continents. His message has reached the corners of the earth, from the farthest west to the remotest east He is accepted as the Promised Guided Leader and the Promised Messiah of the Second Advent in the Americas, in Europe, in Africa, in Asia and even in the distant islands of the Southeast Pacific, such as Fiji, Tuvalu, Solomon Islands etc. Despite this, his followers can best be described as a small pool insignificant in volume as compared to the large sea of the Christian world.

The achievements of Ḥaḍrat Mirza Ghulam Aḥmad's[as] Movement would require an account too lengthy for the small space available here but it is essential to note that no other religious movement in the modern times has progressed and spread so rapidly with such a firm step. It is not a cult, nor is it a popular craze. It is a serious message, an uphill task which requires great effort and discipline on the part of those who venture to follow it. Those who follow it do so by accepting grave responsibilities that are to be discharged throughout their lives. It is almost as austere as the early Essene society. To accept Ḥaḍrat Mirza Ghulam Aḥmad's[as] claim as the Promised Messiah is not hobnobbing with romance, but is a commitment of a lifetime. Those who get initiated in his Community have to deny most of the vain pleasures of their lives, not in the style of the ascetics and the hermits, but with a deep conviction, commitment, satisfaction and contentment of heart that enables them to sacrifice and persevere in his cause to a high degree of excellence. He has created a worldwide community which has no equal in financial sacrifice. All earning members of the Community commit themselves to pay at least a sixteenth of their income towards the noble cause. The spirit of voluntary sacrifice and the amount of voluntary labour which is performed throughout the world is mind boggling. Yet all this is done without the least coercion of any type. Those who are able to put in their share of labour or financial offerings consider themselves fortunate to be able to do so.

This is a community that is entirely independent in its financial affairs. This universal system of voluntary contribution is being exercised for the last hundred years with remarkable purity and moral integrity. Therein lies the secret of its success in maintaining its independence from outside influences for over a century. That, however, is only one angle of observation. Looking at the quality of his followers from other angles provides no less a fascinating scenario. It is a community which stands out in its moral peaceful co-existence, mutual love and deep respect for human values. It is a religious community that is highly admired the world over for its respect of law and regard for decent human relationships irrespective of religion, colour or creed.

To a reader it may seem that we have out-stepped into a track, which has no relationship to the subject of our address. Let us most respectfully point out that such an observer has missed the point. The relevance of this discussion can be better understood in the light of a profound observation of Jesus Christ^{as} that the tree is known by its fruit. (Matt 12:33)

If anyone today is seriously interested in determining the bona fides of Ḥaḍrat Mirza Ghulam Aḥmad's claim, this is the best and the most dependable criterion. On this criterion it can be judged whether he is indeed that Promised Messiah^{as} whose advent had been foretold not only by Jesus Christ^{as} himself but also by the Holy Founder^{sa} of Islam. To discover what manner of followers he has been able to produce and what the passage of a century has done to them would be a very rewarding exercise. The question would also arise whether they have been treated by the age in a manner similar to the followers of Jesus Christ^{as} in the first century of Christianity? Again the question must arise as to what was the attitude of God towards Ḥaḍrat Mirza Ghulam Aḥmad^{as} in the face of the many attempts that were made to annihilate and exterminate him and his Community? Has the attitude of God been in favour of, or has it been against, such a hunted community? If like the early Christians, the followers of Ḥaḍrat Mirza Ghulam Aḥmad^{as} too has been experiencing the same pressing support of God against all odds, if whenever they were ground through the mill of persecution, instead of being pulverised, they emerged on the other end even larger than before and more powerful and more respected, then of course the claim of such a claimant cannot be trivially waived. It is no longer the tall claim of a madman, or a fanciful cobweb of a daydreamer's imagination. Aḥmadiyyat has become a reality to be taken seriously on a much wider horizon than Christianity could ever have been taken towards the end of its first century.

Here is the case of a Messiah[as] who was a fact of history and not the product of fiction, and here again is the case of a Messiah[as] whose re-advent was as realistic as was his first appearance as a commissioned Divine leader. It is entirely up to the people of this age to choose to live continuously in a world of legends and fancies and to keep eternally awaiting the promised reformers of their religions and creeds or to accept the hard realities of this life. On one thing we must agree, that many a religious leader has been elevated from the common human ranks to the ranks of deities. Many a time, religious leaders have been imagined to have ascended to heaven to await somewhere in the empty recesses of space for their second visit to the planet Earth. There is no reason why one should accept one such claim and reject another, because they are merely claims, without any positive, scientific proof to support their validity. Hence there is no option but to either accept them all, or to reject them in their entirety. This would be the only honest and just course of action. One thing however is certain, that once departed from their terrestrial existence, regard-less of the manner in which their followers believed them to have departed, never in the entire history of mankind have any of them ever revisited the Earth. Again, it is most certain that all such divines and spiritual leaders, who have been elevated to the status of deities or partners of God, began their lives like ordinary humble human beings and lived until their deaths the life of a human. It was only their followers who turned them into gods. But remember that none of them ever demonstrated his role in the running of nature. There has always been only One Hand which seems to govern the laws of nature. The mirror of the heavens and the laws of nature at every level reflect the face of One God and One God alone. The Holy Quran says:

$$\text{وَقَالُوااتَّخَذَ الرَّحْمٰنُ وَلَدًا ۚ لَقَدْ جِئْتُمْ شَيْئًا اِدًّا ۚ}$$

$$\text{تَكَادُ السَّمٰوٰتُ يَتَفَطَّرْنَ مِنْهُ وَتَنْشَقُّ الْاَرْضُ وَتَخِرُّ الْجِبَالُ هَدًّا ۚ}$$

$$\text{اَنْ دَعَوْا لِلرَّحْمٰنِ وَلَدًا ۚ وَمَا يَنْبَغِى لِلرَّحْمٰنِ اَنْ يَّتَّخِذَ وَلَدًا ۚ}$$

'They allege: The Gracious One has taken unto Himself a son. Assuredly, you have uttered a monstrous thing! The heavens might well-nigh burst thereat, and the earth cleave asunder, and the mountains fall down to pieces, because they ascribe a son to the Gracious One; whereas it becomes not the Gracious One to take unto Himself a son.' (The Holy Quran 19:89–93)

CHAPTER NINE

CONCLUSION

As FAR AS THIS ENQUIRY IS CONCERNED, we hope that we have done enough justice to it. But before we rest our case here we want to make a passionate appeal to the Christian world to get down from their ivory tower of make-belief and descend to the hard realities of life. Jesus Christ[as] was a perfect man in the context of his age, but no more than a man. He reached the heights which he was destined to reach as a special Messenger of God, entitled the Messiah[as]. This made him unique among all the prophets since the time of Moses[as] to the time of his advent.

Every Prophet is assigned a difficult task indeed. They have to bring about reformation among a people that have become thoroughly evil. In the case of Jesus[as], this task was made even more difficult because he was not only to fight against the common evils of society, but he was to bring about a dramatic and revolutionary change in the attitude of the Jewish people.

As it happens in the case of followers of every religion, with the passage of time they gradually deviate away from truth and begin to wander in the wilderness of sin. So did it happen in the case of the Jewish people. By the time of the advent of Jesus[as], they had virtually become spiritually dead. The water of divine life had ebbed out, leaving behind dead stony hearts. The task Jesus[as] was assigned was to transform them once again into living pulsating human hearts and to bring forth from them springs of human kindness. This was the miracle Jesus[as] wrought and therein lies his greatness.

Now that the world of Islam and Christianity are jointly awaiting the second advent of Jesus Christ[as], they must not forget that the Jesus[as] who was destined to come had to be essentially the same Jesus[as] in character and style of mission. However, according to the prophecies of the founder of Islam, Ḥaḍrat Muḥammad[sa], this Jesus[as] was to appear in his second advent not in the world of Christianity but in the world of Islam. Yet the great miracle he was to bring about was to be the same. But this time it was to be the hearts of the Muslims of the latter days, which he would be assigned to transform. This understanding of his second advent is fully supported by some other prophecies of the Holy Prophet[sa]. He predicted that the state of the people of Islam, during the latter days, would be so similar to that of the Jewish people during their decadent period, as one of a pair of shoes is similar to the other of the same pair.

Hence, if the disease was to be the same, the remedy should have been the same as well. The Messiah[as] had to return to the world in the same humble style, not in person, but in spirit and in character, and this is exactly what has happened and has taken place. Such divine and revolutionary persons are always born as insignificant and humble human beings and live a life of humility. They spiritually revisit the earth in exactly the same style and are treated again with the same callousness, prejudice and fanatic hostility. They are never easily recognised as the true representatives of those who had promised their revisit.

What happened to Christ^{as} in his first appearance at the hands of the Jews was bound to happen to him again, but this time at the hands of the Muslims and the Christians who were expecting his return. The same distorted and unreal expectations regarding the way he was to revisit the earth, the same imaginary goals he was expected to pursue, the same unrealistic views of his performance and his achievements on earth as were displayed by the Jewish people of the time of Jesus Christ^{as} were to be repeated by the Muslims during his second advent, and in this way history was to re-enact itself.

Looking back now, one is in a better position to understand the failure of the Jews to recognise their Messiah. We can easily understand their difficulty and draw lessons from their tragedy. Their literal understanding of the scriptures misled them. All this has already been discussed, but to emphasise this important issue, we once again refer to it. It always happens in the history of expected religious Reformers that the people who await them most often than not fail to recognise them because the signs of their recognition are misread and misunderstood. Realities are mythified and metaphors are taken literally.

Almost the same story has been repeated at the time of the Second Advent of the Messiah, Ḥaḍrat Mirza Ghulam Aḥmad^{as} of Qadian. Like the case of the promised descent of Elijah^{as} from the heavens as was awaited by the Jews of Christ's^{as} time someone was again expected to bodily descend from heaven, this time the Messiah himself.

In the case of the Jews, they were expecting the Messiah to come in the state of glory, and usher them into a new era of domination and ascendancy over their Roman masters. All these expectations were shattered by Jesus[as] of Nazareth. When he appeared at last, he appeared to be far removed and distant from the expected image of the advent of Messiah which Jews had been dearly entertaining for centuries.

Strikingly similar events have taken place in relation to the advent of Christ[as] in the person of Ḥaḍrat Mirza Ghulam Aḥmad of Qadian. The role played by his opponents is the same, only the names differ.

The mainstream of the Muslims and the Christians alike have acquired the role of the Jews of the time of Jesus[as]. The objections are the same. The logic of rejection is the same. Yet God treated this humble man with even greater signs of His support than He did the Jesus[as] of the previous age and helped him spread his message far more rapidly in a far greater number of countries and in all the continents of the world. These are the facts, which speak for themselves, but only for those who listen. These are the facts, which are becoming more and more apparent with the passage of time, but only for those who care to observe. Again, the spirit of the messianic message in the context of the contemporary attitudes of the Muslims and the Christians is no different. But only they will understand who do not shut their eyes.

In the end, let us remind, in the prophetic words of Ḥaḍrat Mirza Ghulam Aḥmad[as] of Qadian—the Divinely appointed Messiah of the latter days,—the Christians and the Muslims, who are awaiting the reappearance of Christ[as] for the last so many centuries that:

'Remember very well that no one shall ever come down from heaven. All our opponents who are alive today shall die and none from them shall ever see Jesus[as] son of Mary[as] coming down from heaven; then their children that are left after them shall also die and none from among them shall ever see Jesus[as] son of Mary[as] coming down from heaven and then their third generation shall also die and they, too, shall not see the son of Mary[as] coming down. Then God shall cause great consternation in their minds and they shall then say that even the age of the domination of the Cross has passed away and the way of life has changed completely, yet the son of Mary[as] has not come down. Then in dismay the wise among them shall forsake this belief and three centuries from now shall not have passed when those who await the coming of Jesus[as] son of Mary[as], whether they be Muslims or Christians, shall relinquish altogether this conception.'[*]

So you may wait until a new generation is born, and they will also wait until they have run their course and a new generation would take over. This state of waiting may continue till the end of the time, but no Jesus[as] will bodily descend from heaven. The dreams of his personal visit will never come true, no matter how much those who wait crave him to return. They may even build a wailing wall for themselves as the Jews did more than three

---

[*] *Tadhkiratul-Shahadatain, Ruhani Khzain,* Vol. 20, p. 67

thousand years ago. And they may go on striking their heads against it. But as it happened in the case of the Jews so will it happen again. They will see no messiah descend despite their wailing and torment, generation after generation after generation. Their future expectations of Christ^{as} will produce nothing but emptiness and a void that will never end. This is an utterly bleak prospect indeed.

As for the Christians who really take Christ^{as} to be a literal son of God, let us end this discussion with the warning words from the Holy Quran, the divinely revealed book to the Holy Prophet^{sa} of Islam. It lays out the purposes of his advent:

وَيُنْذِرَ الَّذِيْنَ قَالُوا اتَّخَذَ اللهُ وَلَدَاۗ مَا لَهُمْ بِهٖ مِنْ عِلْمٍ وَّلَا لِاٰبَآئِهِمْ ۚ كَبُرَتْ كَلِمَةً تَخْرُجُ مِنْ اَفْوَاهِهِمْ ؕ اِنْ يَّقُوْلُوْنَ اِلَّا كَذِبًا ۝

He (the holy messenger of Allah) came to warn those who attributed a son to God. They possess no knowledge (of that) nor their forefathers have any. It is an enormity uttered by their mouths. They utter nought but falsehood. (The Holy Quran 18:5–6)

APPENDIX I

A selected list of books containing a mention of *Marhami 'Isā*, and a statement that the ointment was prepared for Jesus[as], i.e., for the wounds of his body. Please note that the total number of books which record this fact number more than a thousand.

Qānūn, by Shaikh-ul-Ra'is Bu 'Ali Sina, Vol.III, page 133.

Sharaḥ Qānūn, by 'Allama Qutb-ud-Din Shirazi, Vol. III.

Kāmil-uṣ-Ṣanā'ah, by 'Ali Bin-Al-'Abbas Al-Majusi, Vol. III, page 602.

Kitāb Majmū'i Baqā'i, Mahmud Muhammad Isma'il Mukhatib, az Khaqan Bakhatab pidar Muhammad Baqa Khan, Vol. II, page 497.

Kitāb Tadhkara'ulul Albāb, by Shaikh Da'ud-ul-Darir-Al-Antaki, page 303.

Qarābādīni Rūmī, compiled about the time of Jesus[as] and translated in the reign of Mamun al-Rashid into Arabic, see Skin Diseases.

Kitāb 'Umdat-ul-Muhtāj, by Ahmad Bin Hasan al-Rashidi al-Hakim. In this book, *Marhami 'Isā*, and other preparations have been noted from a hundred, perhaps more than a hundred books, all these books being in French.

Kitāb Qarābādin, in Persian, by Hakim Muhammad Akbar Arzani—Skin Diseases.

Shifā'ul Asqām, Vol. II, page 230.

Mir'atush Shifā, by Hakim Nathu Shah—(manuscript) Skin Diseases.

Dhakhīra'i Khawārizm Shāhī, Skin Diseases.

Sharaḥ Qānūn Gilānī, Vol. III.

Sharaḥ Qānūn Qarshī, Vol. III.

Qarābādīn, by 'Ulwi Khan, Skin Diseases.

Kitāb 'Ilāj-ul-Amrāḍ, by Hakim Muhammad Sharif Khan Sahib, page 893.

Qarābādīn Yūnānī, Skin Diseases.

Tuḥfat-ul-Mu'minīn, on the margin of Makhzan-ul-Adwiya, page 713.

Kitāb Muḥīt Fiṭ Ṭib, page 367.

'Aksiri A'ẓam, Vol. IV, by Hakim Muhammad A'ẓam Khan Sahib, Al-Mukhatab ba Nazimi Jahan, page 331.

Kitāb Qarābādīn, by Ma'sumi-ul-Ma'sum bin Karim-ud-Din Al-Shustri Shirazi.

Kitāb 'Ijālai Nafi'ah, Muhammad Sharif Dehlavi, page 410.

Kītābi Shibrī, otherwise known as Lawami' Shibriyya, Sayyid Hussain Shibr Kazimi, page 471.

Kitāb Makhzani Sulaimānī, translation of Aksiri 'Arabi, page 599, by Muhammad Shams-ud-Din Sahib of Bahawalpur.

Shifā-'ul-Amrāḍ, translated by Maulana Al-Hakim Muhammad Nur Karim 282.

Kitāb-ul-Ṭibb, Dārā Shakuhī, by Nur-ud-Din Muhammad 'Abdul Hakim, 'Ain-ul-Mulk Al-Shirazi, page 360.

Minhāj-ud-Dukkān ba Dastūr-ul-A'yān fi A'māl wa Tarkīb al Nāfi'ah lil Abdān, by Aflatuni Zamana wa Ra'isi Awana 'Abul Mina Ibni Abi Nasr-ul 'Attar Al-Isra'ili Al-Haruni (i.e., Jew), page 86.

Kitāb Zubdatuṭ Ṭibb,, by Sayyid-ul-Imam Abu Ibrahim Isma'il bin Hasan-ul-Husaini Al-Tarjani, page 182.

Kitāb Ṭibbi Akbar, by Muhammad Akbar Arzani, page 242.

Kitāb Mīzanuṭ Ṭibb, by Muhammad Akbar Arzani, page 152.

Sadīdī, by Ra'isul Mutakallimin Imamul Muhaqq-i-qin Al-Sadid-ul-Kadhruni, Vol. II, page 283.

Kitāb Hadī Kabīr, by Ibni Dhakariyya, Skin Diseases.

Qarābādīn, by Ibni Talmidh, Skin Diseases. *

---

* Above list taken from Jesus in India by Hadrat Mirza Ghulam Alunadas of Qadian, The Promised Messiah, page 56-57.

APPENDIX II

Parthenogenesis; non-sexual reproduction that is the development of the ovum into an individual without fertilization by a spermatozoon.

Parthenogenesis is very common in the insect world and in fish, and is routine in animals such as the aphids. Among the reptiles there is strong evidence that parthenogenesis can be a successful strategy for lizards in an environment with low and unpredictable rainfall[6]. In the Lancet in 1955 it was reported that a woman had a daughter where parthenogenesis could not be disproved. It has been produced in mammals experimentally. There is, however, no certain record of the birth of a parthenogenetic mammal: The most that has been achieved is that parthenogenetic mice and rabbit embryos have developed normally to about halfway through pregnancy but have then died and been aborted.

In humans a recent research study was carried out on 'The development and systematic study of the parthenogenetic activation and early development of human oocyte'.[7] In this study, human oocyte, both freshly retrieved and remaining unfertilized after exposure to spermatozoa, were exposed to alcohol or calcium ionophore and examined for evidence of activation. The outcome of this study was that human oocyte can be activated partheno

---

[6] *Genetics*: 1991 Sept 129(1):211–9
[7] *Fertility—Sterility*—1991 Nov; 56(5):904–12

genetically using calcium ionophore, but at lower rates than seen for mouse oocyte. Human parthenotes can complete division to the 8-cell stage. This data raises the possibility that some early human pregnancy losses may involve oocyte that have been parthenogenetically activated spontaneously.

An incident of partial parthenogenesis in a human was reported in the *New Scientist* of 7 October, 1995 under the heading, '*The boy whose blood has no father*'.[8] In the case of males all cells should have a Y chromosome, but in this particular case study of a three year old boy the white blood cells were found to contain only XX chromosomes. The reporter also mentions that occasionally, chromosomal females carry one X chromosome which includes the maleness gene and that the researchers had at first assumed that their case study was an example of this syndrome. But when they used extremely sensitive DNA technology they were not able to detect any Y chromosome material in the boy's white blood cells. However, the boy's skin was discovered to be genetically different from his blood, having both X and Y chromosomes.

A more detailed analysis of the X chromosomes in the boy's skin and blood revealed that all his X chromosomes were identical and derived entirely from his mother. Similarly, both members of each of the 22 other chromosome pairs in his blood were identical, coming entirely from the mother. The explanation given by the researchers

---

[8] This report concerned the research of David Bonthron et al. and refers to the Oct. 1995 issue of *Nature Genetics* where their report is to be found.

for this phenomenon is that the unfertilised ovum self-activated and began dividing itself into identical cells; one of these cells was then fertilised by a spermatozoon from the father and the resultant mixture of cells began to develop as a normal embryo.

This illustrates that cells created parthenogenetically in mammals are not always disabled. In the case of this boy they were able to create a normal blood system.

Hermaphroditism; a sex anomaly in which gonads for both sexes are present; the external genitalia show traits of both sexes and chromosomes show male female mosaicism (xx/xy).

In a study in the Netherlands in 1990 called 'Combined Hermaphroditism and Auto-fertilization in a Domestic Rabbit,' a true hermaphrodite rabbit served several females and sired more than 250 young of both sexes. In the next breeding season, the rabbit which was housed in isolation, became pregnant and delivered seven healthy young of both sexes. It was kept in isolation and when autopsied was again pregnant and demonstrated two functional ovaries and two infertile testes. A chromosome preparation revealed a diploid number of autosomes and two sex chromosomes of uncertain configuration.

A study was carried out on a human hermaphrodite at the Department of Obstetrics and Gynaecology, Chicago, Lying-in Hospital, Illinois.[9] The objective of this research was to determine the conceptional events resulting in a 46xx, 46xy true hermaph-

---

[9] *Journal of Fertility and Sterility*— JC: evf 57(2): 346–9 1992 Feb.

rodite and to report the first pregnancy in a 46xx, 46xy true hermaphrodite with an ovotestis.

The design of this study involved chromosome studies performed on patient's lymphocytes and fibroblasts, red cell antigens, human leucocytes antigens and the presence of y-chromosome deoxyribonucleic acid were analysed. Findings were compared with parental and sibling blood group data.

The result of these studies demonstrated that our patient is a chimera; an organism in which there are at least two kinds of tissue differing in their genetic constitution, thus with dual maternal and paternal contributions. In addition, despite the presence of an ovotestis, she conceived and delivered a child.

INDEX

It is not the business of any Christian writer or preacher to dilute Christianity to suit the general educated public. The doctrine of the incarnation was to the Jews a stumbling block and to the Greeks foolishness, and so will it always be, for the doctrine not only transcends reason; it the paradox par excellence; and it can be affirmed only by faith, with passionate inwardness and interest The substitution of reason for faith means the death of Christianity.

—Keirkegaard